ABOUT ISLAND PRESS

Island Press is the only nonprofit organization in the United States whose principal purpose is the publication of books on environmental issues and natural resource management. We provide solutions-oriented information to professionals, public officials, business and community leaders, and concerned citizens who are shaping responses to environmental problems.

In 2000, Island Press celebrates its sixteenth anniversary as the leading provider of timely and practical books that take a multidisciplinary approach to critical environmental concerns. Our growing list of titles reflects our commitment to bringing the best of an expanding body of literature to the environmental community throughout North America and the world.

Support for Island Press is provided by The Jenifer Altman Foundation, The Bullitt Foundation, The Mary Flagler Cary Charitable Trust, The Nathan Cummings Foundation, The Geraldine R. Dodge Foundation, The Charles Engelhard Foundation, The Ford Foundation, The German Marshall Fund of the United States, The George Gund Foundation, The Vira I. Heinz Endowment, The William and Flora Hewlett Foundation, The W. Alton Jones Foundation, The John D. and Catherine T. MacArthur Foundation, The Andrew W. Mellon Foundation, The Charles Stewart Mott Foundation, The Curtis and Edith Munson Foundation, The National Fish and Wildlife Foundation, The New-Land Foundation, The Oak Foundation, The Overbrook Foundation, The David and Lucile Packard Foundation, The Pew Charitable Trusts, The Rockefeller Brothers Fund, Rockefeller Financial Services, The Winslow Foundation, and individual donors.

THE REGIONAL CITY

THE REGIONAL CITY

PETER CALTHORPE
WILLIAM FULTON
FOREWORD BY ROBERT FISHMAN

Island Press
Washington • Covelo • London

Library of Congress Cataloging-in-Publication Data

Calthorpe, Peter.
  The Regional City : planning for the end of sprawl / Peter Calthorpe and William Fulton.
      p. cm.
Includes bibliographical references and index.
  ISBN 1-55963-783-8 (cloth : acid-free paper) — ISBN 1-55963-784-6 (pbk. : acid-free paper)
  1. Regional planning—United States. 2. Land use—United States. 3. Open spaces—United States. 4. Metropolitan areas—United States. I. Fulton, William B., 1955– II. Title
  HT392 .C28 2001
  307.1'216'0973—dc21
                                    00-011978

British Library Cataloguing in Publication Data available.

To my father, who taught me to always question assumptions,
and to my mother, who taught me to study. –P. C.

For Sara Elizabeth Torf Fulton, who works very hard every day
to make the world a better place. –W. F.

CONTENTS

ACKNOWLEDGMENTS

I would like to start these acknowledgments at the professional roots of most of the ideas developed here. It was in Sacramento in the mid-1970s that an extraordinary group of individuals gathered as part of Governor Jerry Brown's administration to rethink much about our society. In that group, with which I had the opportunity to work, were Sim Van der Ryn and Bill Press. Bill, as head of the Office of Planning and Research, developed the "Urban Strategy" for the state of California, an effort and a set of strategies that quite simply lays out much of the thesis of the Regional City at the metropolitan scale—twenty-five years ago. It was never adopted. Sim, who was to become my partner and mentor, was state architect and focused on the complex relation among buildings, community, and ecology. Much of his thinking has found its way into my work on neighborhood design and a concern for the environmental consequences of development. Also of that time was an old friend and architectural professor of mine from Yale, David Sellers, who worked with us on our first experiments in urban infill and intensification. Dave has inspired many, including me, with his spirit, humor, and inventiveness in the many design charrettes that followed over the next two decades.

Doug Kelbaugh, now dean at the School of Architecture at the University of Michigan, and Harrison Fraker, dean at the School of Environmental Design UC–Berkeley, were lasting friends and co-conspirators in our efforts through the late 1970s and early 1980s to fashion an environmentally responsible form of architecture. Doug became my partner in developing a first rough idea about suburban growth called the pedestrian pocket. From that point on, as both friend and collaborator, he has helped articulate and invent much of the community-planning concepts that underlie the Regional City. It was through design experimentation at the School of Environmental Design at Berkeley that these hypothetical ideas continued to germinate. Dan Solomon and Lars Lerup supported and participated in studios that questioned and refined the notion of redesigning the suburbs. Dan has remained over the years a close collaborator and friend, as well as my architectural conscience.

Just as the 1980s ended, these ideas—dormant and theoretical—opened up with the support of an enlightened developer named Phil Angelides, now California State Treasurer. Phil had the vision and the guts to experiment with a major development, and attempt to shape a more diverse and walkable community at Laguna West. In that project I found another close friend and compatriot in Ken Kay, a landscape designer of rare talent who in every project teaches me something new about the subtleties of place making. Simultaneously, several local politicians, most notably Grantland Johnson (then county supervisor, now secretary of California's Health and Human Services Agency), supported an effort to rezone Sacramento County for Transit Oriented Development—a first pass at reorganizing the suburbs with transit and mixed-use communities.

Soon thereafter, Henry Richmond, the inspired leader of 1000 Friends of Oregon, launched a radical alternative for regional growth in Portland that succeeded in redefining the debate about growth in that region. His vision and leadership set the foundation for Portland's transformation into a Regional City. John Fregonese complimented Henry's work in his 2040 Plan for Metro. In working for John on the plan, I had the opportunity to make a lifelong friend and, ultimately, gain a professional partner who knows more about regional design than anyone I know. He has the unique capacity to humanize complex regional strategies, to bring together disparate groups into rare coalitions, and to communicate grand visions simply and clearly. Together we helped develop the regional vision for Salt Lake and in every project we pursue, I am honored to be working with him.

By the early 1990s, more and more designers were rethinking the shape of community. Some came together in 1992 to form the Congress for New Urbanism (CNU). I am deeply indebted to the founders of the CNU—Andres Duany, Liz Plater-

Zyberk, Stefanos Polyzoides, Elizabeth Moule, and Dan Solomon—for providing a remarkable forum in which ideas could cross-fertilize, and for creating a set of friendships and a sense of comradery that helps to sustain both a national movement and my personal growth. I owe much to many others within the CNU, such as Robert Davis, the developer of Seaside, Hank Dittmar, formerly head of STTP, Bill Morrish, head of the Design Center for the American Urban Landscape, and John Norquist, mayor of Milwaukee, for their commitment to principles and their willingness to set aside personal time for the sake of advancing a cause in which we all believe.

At the core of these acknowledgments must be my current and past co-workers at Calthorpe Associates (CA). Without them, the ideas here would not have developed in practice; through them, our work becomes more unique, diverse, and compelling. Joe Scanga was the first employee of CA, and is now one of its Principles and remains in a special way the heart and soul of our practice. Matt Taecker, also a Principle, joined not long after Joe and has become one of the most accomplished and skillful community designers I know. More recently, Tim Rood has become a central leader in the firm, combining planning skills at the regional level with a keen sense of design at the local level. I am indebted to Phil Erickson and Shelley Poticha—two past members of our practice who have moved on to different challenges. They helped guide the work in our early years and contributed greatly to the emerging field of regional design. Phil has since started his own practice and Shelley has become the executive director of the CNU. In this role, she has done an extraordinary job of expanding the agenda and influence of a fledgling organization—and she has done it with endless reserves of energy, goodwill, and good judgment.

Creating this book was a team effort with my coauthor Bill Fulton and several others. Bill brought just the right mix of knowledge, writing skills, and personal experience to broaden the message and clarify the definition of the Regional City. I am particularly indebted to Bill for our intense debates that always served to advance the depth of thinking and (I hope) strength of argument present in the book. Heather Boyer, our ever patient and supportive editor at Island Press, shaped this work in many unseen ways—introducing Bill and me, pushing us on content and concepts, and helping us with final edits. Marianna Leuschel and the entire L Studio team designed and produced a book that not only is elegant but also reflects the content in many subtle ways. In this work they went way beyond the call of duty in applying their extraordinary talents.

My family and extended family are the true foundation of this work. Without their support and love, not much of this would have come to pass. Jean Driscoll, my wife, and Diana Rose, my sister, saw me through critical surgery in the midst of completing this book—just one of many lifesaving manifestations of their love and generosity. Jeannie and my brother-in-law Jonathon Rose are also indirect professional companions—Jonathon, in his role as progressive developer, always challenges my thinking and calls on me to always push beyond any design formula. Jeannie, with her background in affordable housing and land preservation, lends me knowledge and perspective it would take a lifetime to accumulate. My children—Lucia, Jacob, and Asa—constantly remind me why better communities are essential and how we must all lead more balanced lives.

PETER CALTHORPE
Berkeley, California
August 2000

My greatest debt goes to my colleague Peter Calthorpe, who graciously asked me to work with him in writing this book.

I have always admired the founders of the New Urbanism movement for their commitment, their vision, and their ability to give voice to feelings so many of us in urban planning have had over the last twenty years about what is wrong with the built environment and what could make it better. But my admiration for Peter goes much deeper than that. From the beginning, Peter has never viewed the street or the block in isolation; rather, he has always sought to understand the relationship between the block and the metropolis as a whole, and to illuminate for all of us how this relationship affects the way we live our daily lives. That is the essence of what our book is about, and I hope that our joint effort here does justice to Peter's admirable vision.

I am also very grateful to many other people who have helped and inspired me over the years in seeking to understand the Regional City, either through conversation or by providing me opportunities to conduct research that has deepened my knowledge.

Will Fleissig of Continuum Partners in Denver first introduced me to these concepts as one of my planning school professors many years ago, and he remains a dear friend. Michael Mantell, now of Resources Law Group in Sacramento, has provided me with similar insight and inspiration over the years, and Jeanne Sedgwick and Mark Valentine of The Packard Foundation have given me innumerable opportunities to work on these issues. Alan Ehrenhalt of *Governing* magazine and Bob McNulty of Partners for Livable Communities have provided both stimulating conversation and many opportunities to research these issues. Bruce Katz and the Brookings Institution's Center for Urban and Metropolitan Policy have provided an excellent national forum to discuss metropolitan growth.

I have gained great insight into regional issues from Robert E. Lang of the Fannie Mae Foundation, John Landis of UC Berkeley, Rolf Pendall of Cornell University, Manuel Pastor of UC Santa Cruz, and Bill Barnes of the National League of Cities. Madelyn Glickfeld and Tom Horan of the late, great Claremont Graduate School Research Institute inspired me and helped me understand the Regional City closest to my home, Los Angeles. More recently, Michael Dear and Jennifer Wolch of the Southern California Studies Center at the University of Southern California have done the same, and I am grateful to them and to their research assistants for their inspiration and support.

Many thanks as well to Myron Orfield of the Metropolitan Areas Research Corp. in Minneapolis, who actually read the entire manuscript and commented thoughtfully on it; to Carol Whiteside of the Great Valley Center in Modesto, who first understood California's Central Valley as a Regional City, and to Mary McCumber of the Puget Sound Regional Council and Mark Hinshaw of LMN Architects for putting up with repeated pestering about Seattle. For our sections on Consolidated Planning and HOPE VI, both Peter and I received a great deal of assistance from many people at the U.S. Department of Housing and Urban Development, led by Susan Wachter, the Assistant Secretary for Policy Development and Research, and Elinor Bacon, the Deputy Assistant Secretary for Public Housing Investments.

Heather Boyer of Island Press was both patient and persistent in seeing the manuscript through to completion. I am always thankful for the work of Robert Fishman. Not only did Bob agree to write the foreword, but he has, over many years, framed the question of metropolitan growth in the United States with remarkable grace and clarity. And I can never repay my enormous debt to the late K. C. Parsons, who let me share his cavernous office at Cornell and spent many hours discussing Clarence Stein and the early regionalists. K. C., I miss you very much.

Closer to home, I could not have completed this project without a great deal of help from my colleagues at Solimar Research Group in Ventura. Alicia Harrison and Peter Sezzi performed the often thankless task of gathering and organizing a vast amount of background material. Paul Shigley took on added editorial duties at California Planning & Development Report so that I could devote more time to this book. Mary Molina provided crucial logistical support to ensure that both I and my words were always in the right place at the right time. Thanks to all of you.

Many thanks as well to the staff of Calthorpe Associates in Berkeley, especially Joe DiStefano, who bailed me out of impossible problems on numerous occasions. Peter and Jean Driscoll put me up (or put up with me, depending on how you look at it) at their house in Berkeley more times than I can count. And the folks at Café Coffee in Ventura allowed me to park myself on their comfortable sofa for hours at a time while working on this book.

As always, I owe more than I can say to my wife, Vicki Torf Fulton, and my daughter, Sara Elizabeth Torf Fulton. They have lived with this book and its ideas—as well as my frequent absences—for a long time. But they both continue to inspire me every day to help create a world that is kind, fair, and fun. And what more can you ask of the Regional City than that?

WILLIAM FULTON
Ventura, California
August 2000

FOREWORD

A century ago the United States faced the challenge of the industrial city. Vast centers like New York and Chicago, larger than any cities in history, were growing faster than any in history, teeming with an unassimilated immigrant population and prey to disease, poverty, and social conflict. Nevertheless, these cities became in the first half of the twentieth century the heartlands of American prosperity and global power.

Today the challenge is what Peter Calthorpe and William Fulton call the Regional City. The industrial cities of the early twentieth century have evolved into our twenty-first-century "metropolitan regions," sprawling agglomerations of central city and suburbs that could extend a hundred miles in every direction and cover countless political jurisdictions. Where the main problem of the old city had been inhumanly dense concentrations of people and industry, the metropolitan region suffers from "sprawl," the inefficient and environmentally degrading spread of population. Where the old city suffered from very visible forms of smoke and water pollution, the new region is prey to more insidious forms of pollution and the continuing destruction of the natural environment. If poverty is now less widespread than in the old cities, it is also more isolated, more alienated, and more degrading.

The issues raised by these twin crises of sprawl and the inner city are fundamental: the relationship of a technologically advanced society to the natural world and the equally fundamental issue of social equity. Yet these pressing problems have been allowed to fester, with even the most creative responses stymied by fragmented political jurisdictions, by endemic conflicts between cities and their suburbs, and by a federal government whose uncoordinated policies have made regional cooperation difficult. While unsolved problems accumulate, the stakes have grown higher. As national governments decline in their ability to control the global economy, the key units worldwide have become the regions. Metropolitan regions that promote and manage growth, educate their populations, and maintain the quality of life will succeed. Those that remain mired in conflict and inaction will fail.

This book takes up the challenge of the Regional City as the necessary scale on which to confront our society's economic, ecological, and social problems. Calthorpe and Fulton have gotten past those twin towers of negativism—the urban crisis and sub-urban sprawl—to provide a manifesto for all those who see traffic jams, loss of open space, and racial divisions not as necessities to be endured but as problems to be solved. Among recent works on regionalism, this book, in my opinion, is the most comprehensive, the most practical, and the most visionary. As Calthorpe and Fulton announce, the Regional City is "not merely a theory," and they back up this claim with a wonderfully comprehensive selection of project descriptions and graphics from Calthorpe Associates' work. Their discussion of these projects is supported by Calthorpe's practical, hands-on experience in so many of our most creative and important regional initiatives.

Perhaps most crucially, this book is visionary in the sense that the authors insist that an overall regional design vision is necessary for successful action. For Calthorpe and Fulton, regionalism means not only thinking bigger but thinking better. It means seeing the interconnections between, for example, land use and transportation, open space and public space, growth boundaries at the edge of the region and rebuilt inner cities at their core. Where traditional policy analyses tend to separate and obscure these key interconnections, physical design embodies and reveals the links. It provides the common ground around which the different stakeholders in the region can come together for effective action. This book is a powerful argument for the crucial role of regional design as the synthetic discipline bringing together the separate worlds of economics, ecology, social policy, and aesthetics.

The Regional City is therefore filled with designs for the present and the future, but it is also based on a long tradition of American regional thought and planning. A brief comparison between Calthorpe and Fulton and some of their predecessors might help us to understand how this book is both a critique of and a contribution to that tradition.

As early as the 1920s, a remarkable group of architects, planners, and social activists led by Lewis Mumford, Clarence Stein, Henry Wright, and Benton MacKaye had attempted to make the region the primary focus for American planning. As founders of the Regional Planning Association of America (RPAA), they already saw that the new technologies of their time—the automobile, electric power, the telephone, and radio—meant the crisis of the industrial city, or what Clarence Stein called the "dinosaur cities." The need to crowd urban functions inside a single massive dense core at the heart of a region no longer existed. Instead, cities and their citizens could expand throughout the region into that green world of farms and small towns that once seemed to be the inevitable counterpart to urban life.

The leaders of the RPAA saw this coming regional transformation as a source of hope. Properly planned, decentralization could be channeled into New Towns: communities of about thirty thousand people that would include both work and residence, large enough to generate their own urbanity but bordered and contained by a perpetual greenbelt. Spread throughout the region's greenfields, the New Towns would combine efficiency, beauty, and social equity in ways impossible for older cities disfigured by slums and industrial pollution. The "dinosaur cities" would fade away and the new "regional city" would emerge as a network of New Towns in a perpetually green landscape: the home of an advanced society in union with nature.

Sadly, these prophets proved to be exactly half-right. After World War II, the American city decentralized with a vengeance, but the result was not the RPAA's ideal of the regional city. Postwar growth meant not only the expansion of the suburbs but their "urbanization." The central cities fragmented and exploded into a hybrid form that spread low-density development rapidly throughout whole regions and erased the traditional distinctions between city, suburb, and countryside. Contemplating this boundless "anti-city," as he termed it, Lewis Mumford despaired of American society itself.

Calthorpe and Fulton have helped to revive much of the hope and idealism of the earlier regionalists, while learning from the early mistakes and failures. First, the 1920s regionalists perceived the giant city with its slums and congestion as the overwhelming problem, and they looked eagerly to its decline and fall. They little imagined what depopulation and deindustrialization would do to our major urban centers, and especially to the poor left behind. By contrast, Calthorpe and Fulton's regionalism recognizes the crucial role of a robust central city, and they focus particularly in this book on ways to rebuild the inner city. As they argue, the problem of the inner city must be approached as part of a larger regional strategy that includes affordable housing throughout the region, tax-sharing between cities and suburbs, revived mass transit, and regional growth boundaries as a way of directing growth back to the core. But they rightly insist on the role that well-designed, mixed-use urban neighborhoods can play in addressing regional inequities, and their concluding section on the federal HOPE VI projects is perhaps the most important in the book.

Secondly, the early regionalists believed that the self-contained New Town represented the single ideal physical form for an advanced civilization, and they looked forward to the time when the bulk of the American population lived in one. But in fact the full-fledged New Town (represented in this country by Columbia, Maryland, and Reston, Virginia) has proven virtually impossible for private developers to build and difficult even for the welfare states like postwar Britain and Sweden that once attempted them. In any case, the time for utopias has vanished, and so too has the ample open space at the edge of the regions where the 1920s regionalists had hoped to plant their ideal cities. Instead of New Towns on greenfield sites, Calthorpe and Fulton concentrate on suburban infill and redevelopment, the steady work of upgrading the suburban fabric to provide for walkable town centers, mixed-use neighborhoods, and public space.

Finally, the earlier regionalists were still caught up in the great wave of modernist optimism that saw radical innovation as salvation. Only by discarding all past urban forms and embracing the newest technology could the Regional City emerge. The 1920s regionalists were particularly enamored of the automobile, a perspective that Lewis Mumford, especially, lived to regret. Calthorpe and Fulton's twenty-first-century regionalism is built on a far more complex relationship to past and present. As Calthorpe wrote in 1986, "there is a special kind of wisdom in our cities born of time and its shifting forces." Calthorpe and Fulton turn to older urban forms not out of nostalgia or preservationism, but precisely to activate that wisdom as a resource for future innovation. Their aim, as they eloquently state it, is to maintain "some simple and basic urban design principles [which] are (as they always have been) to create places that are walkable and human-scaled, that are diverse in population and varied in uses, and that are shaped around public spaces that are meaningful and memorable."

One sees this commitment most clearly in Calthorpe's most important design concept, "transit-oriented development (TOD)," introduced in his book *The Next American Metropolis* (1993), and central to this one. In regional terms, transit-oriented development means reorienting the region around a system of light-rail lines emanating from a central city hub. Each stop becomes the town center for a mini New Town, a mixed-use community with stores, jobs, and diverse housing, all within walking distance of the transit stop with its links to other towns and downtown. In some respects, Calthorpe and Fulton are rediscovering the "streetcar suburbs" of the turn of the twentieth century. But, in the context of regions where automobile-based development permitted limitless sprawl, transit-oriented development introduces a radical break with the immediate past. Far from reviving a vanished past, the use of this "obsolete" rail technology represents the possibility of a more complex twenty-first-century region.

In one respect, however, Calthorpe and Fulton are directly in the tradition of the earlier regionalists. Mumford, Stein, and their colleagues found it natural to combine the roles of authors, designers, and activists, and Calthorpe and Fulton have also resisted the far stronger pressures of specialization today. This book could only have been written by authors who have been testing and refining their theories over many years and many projects. Those who decry the absence of engaged "public intellectuals" in American life might look carefully at the range and achievements of both authors.

Trained as an architect, Peter Calthorpe has since the 1970s sought an ever widening design synthesis that would integrate urbanism and environmentalism. From designing energy-efficient houses, he moved to designing the compact, sustainable, equitable communities where those houses would find their proper context, and now to designing the regional framework that would support those communities. In all these endeavors Calthorpe has shown an impressive capacity to learn from history and from colleagues, and above all to translate social values into clear and compelling physical form.

In his first book, *Sustainable Communities: A New Design Synthesis for Cities, Suburbs, and Towns* (1986; written and edited with Sim Van der Ryn), Calthorpe had already formulated many of his leading ideas: that suburban sprawl was not only ecologically but socially destructive; and conversely, that the compact urban designs that were most ecologically sustainable were also potentially the most socially valuable. This insight led him to extensive research into the design of pedestrian-friendly, mixed-use communities. Working with architect and educator Doug Kelbaugh, he put forward the plan for what he called a "pedestrian pocket," a "simple cluster of housing, retail spaces and offices within a quarter-mile walking radius of a transit system." The pedestrian pocket exemplifies Calthorpe's critical relationship to the older regionalists.

While drawing on New Town design, he specifically rejects the overambitious scale and stand-alone quality of the full-sized New Town. Indeed, the 50- to 100-acre pedestrian pocket makes sense only through its transit links to other towns and to the regional core. The pedestrian pocket concept is thus a regional plan whose implications Calthorpe would work out in his transit-oriented development.

In 1989, Sacramento developer Phil Angelides turned to Calthorpe Associates (founded in 1983) for the design of Laguna West, a 1,000-acre mixed-use project that Calthorpe called "the first on-the-ground test" of his ideas. That same year, the Sacramento County Planning Department commissioned Calthorpe Associates to produce "transit-oriented development guidelines" for the Sacramento region, a commission that was followed by a similar project for the city of San Diego in 1991. In 1992, the citizens group 1000 Friends of Oregon asked Calthorpe Associates to help provide an alternative to a new freeway slated for the west side of the Portland region. This project, outlined in this book, gave Calthorpe a major voice in the region that was already the most receptive to his ideas. The resulting Land Use Transportation Air Quality Connection (LUTRAQ) became not only the most thorough of his regional plans for transit-oriented development but also the most influential. Not only did LUTRAQ nix the freeway, it led to the implementation of both a new light-rail line and transit-oriented land-use guidelines. Today, Calthorpe Associates along with John Fregonese, new partner and former head of planning for Portland Metro, are deeply engaged in regional planning throughout the country, perhaps most notably in the Envision Utah project that begins this book.

In 1992, Calthorpe and other West Coast designers joined with Andres Duany, Elizabeth Plater-Zyberk, and others from the East Coast to found the Congress for the New Urbanism. The CNU has given Calthorpe a national platform, and his transit-oriented development stands alongside Duany and Plater-Zyberk's "neo-traditional town" as the two central concepts of the movement. Perhaps more important, the CNU has given Calthorpe a venue in which to debate and refine his ideas. (Contrary to the myth, the CNU is less an engine of design orthodoxy than it is a meeting ground for often passionate debate.) Like Duany and Plater-Zyberk, Calthorpe has always emphasized the centrality of the pedestrian-scaled neighborhood in the revitalization of the region, but, compared to them, Calthorpe has been less concerned with rules, codes, definitions, and historical precedents. He continues to revisit and revise his basic concepts, including the changing meaning of the neighborhood in the new regional context.

Coauthor William Fulton has combined a national practice in planning—he is the founder and principal of Solimar Research Group—with equally important achievements as an author. In a field not always distinguished for prose style, Fulton is an accomplished writer who has mastered a variety of forms from the hard-hitting article to the definitive (yet highly readable) *Guide to California Planning.* Editor of the *California Planning and Development Report,* he has also served as chair of the West Hollywood Planning Commission. These varied experiences all contributed to his most notable achievement, his book on the Los Angeles region, *The Reluctant Metropolis: The Politics of Growth in Los Angeles* (1997). Among the many important recent books on contemporary Los Angeles, Fulton's is in my judgment the best. It is also perhaps the best analysis we have of the politics and power struggles of a large American region.

The Reluctant Metropolis shows Los Angeles caught between the crisis of the nation's most powerful growth machine and the difficult emergence of a critical regionalism. Fulton teaches us how the highly fragmented politics of Los Angeles can nevertheless generate immense power within the "shadow government" that controls the massive infrastructure investments in water, electricity, and transportation and operates through little-publicized authorities like the Metropolitan Water District or the Southern California Association of Governments. He also shows the travails of local citizen activism and the difficulties of creating not only a regional consciousness but a regional citizenship. *The Reluctant Metropolis* makes clear the challenges that *The Regional City* must confront.

In his classic of regionalist thought, *The Culture of Cities* (1938), Lewis Mumford grandiloquently proclaimed that the "re-animation and re-building of regions, as deliberate works of collective art, is the grand task of politics for the opening generation." In fact, the generation that Mumford addressed had other pressing tasks, starting with World War II, and the promise of regionalism seemed indefinitely postponed. This book allows us to hope that Mumford's "opening generation" is finally here.

ROBERT FISHMAN
Professor of Architecture
A. Alfred Taubman College of Architecture
University of Michigan

This book describes three interrelated phenomena: the emergence of regionalism,

the maturation of the suburbs, and the revitalization of older urban neighborhoods.

Each is a topic unto itself, but each is now critically dependent on the other two.

INTRODUCTION

In a large conference room in downtown Salt Lake City overlooking the city that Brigham Young laid out some 153 years ago, civic leaders gather to begin the process of envisioning the future of their fast-growing region. The city that was once a precursor to the American dream—each home on a one-acre lot bounded by streets wide enough for a U-turn by a horse and carriage—has evolved into blocks of parking lots, scattered mid-rise buildings, and six-lane streets recently punctuated with a new light-rail line. The 150 participants sit at small tables in groups of 10, armed with detailed maps of the region and seventy "chips"—small squares of paper, each representing four square miles of typical suburban growth. Their assignment: to accommodate the next million people in Salt Lake City by finding the best way to arrange the chips on the map.

At one of the tables, Utah Governor Mike Leavitt joins a random group that includes the head of a local environmental group, a major housing developer, a small-city mayor, and other community representatives. First, they lay the chips side by side in classic suburban fashion. But soon the chips have covered almost all of the region's dwindling agricultural land. Then they look for other buildable pieces of land and begin laying the chips on pristine mountain plateaus, accessible to Salt Lake City only through scenic mountain passes. The participants at the governor's table—and throughout the room—soon realize that if the Salt Lake region continues to grow at the current densities, much of what they love about the Wasatch Front will be destroyed.

So each group takes a different approach. Instead of spreading the chips out, the participants begin stacking them, one on top of the other—indicating that they are willing to accept higher densities in order to preserve agriculture and pristine land. When that isn't enough, they begin laying the chips on top of existing urban areas—in places that they know are underbuilt or in need of renewal. By the time they are done, they recognize that a different vision of their future is necessary and possible.

In the months that follow, this group and many others discover that a sprawling future for the Salt Lake area will be harmful in other ways. They learn that, compared with a more compact alternative, low-density sprawl will cost as much as an additional $15 billion in infrastructure and public services—approximately $30,000 for every new household. They learn that, even with a massive road-building effort, traffic congestion and air pollution will only get worse. They find that current zoning policies won't accommodate the region's growing number of senior citizens, singles, and young families in the years ahead. Perhaps most painful of all for such a family-oriented region, Salt Lake's civic leaders conclude that many of their children will not be able to afford to live in the Salt Lake area.

In other words, they find that "more of the same" will not solve their problems. Twelve months after sitting down at the table with the map and the chips, Governor Leavitt signs the Quality Growth Initiative—Utah's first growth-management law. In the Salt Lake City area, "sprawl as usual" is suddenly a thing of the past.

THE LIFE AND DEATH OF EDGE CITIES

Sprawl means different things to different people. To some, it is the honest expression of who we are—fractured, free, and consumptive. To others, it is a virus infecting the land and our culture. We believe it is a model of development that is simply past its time. It was a postwar strategy to house a growing middle class in low-density places knitted together by the car. This pattern once delivered affordable single-family homes, low crime, open space, and free access for the car. Now homes are distant and more expensive, crime spreads, open space recedes, and cars are stuck in traffic. Sprawl now seems at once outdated and, for many, increasingly unaffordable.

"Edge Cities" are defined by Joel Garreau in his seminal book *Edge City: Life on the New Frontier* as suburban areas complete with major job centers and regional retail. It is an accurate description of our contemporary regions and an apt name. For the first time, suburbs are the nexus of our culture and economy. In many cases, the focus of commerce and creative enterprise has shifted away from cities.

As the suburbs progressed from the bedroom communities of the 1950s and 1960s to these contemporary Edge Cities, many fundamental changes took place—changes that now dominate our identity, our politics, our opportunities, and our sense of community. We changed from a country of villages, towns, and cities to a country of subdivisions, malls, and office parks. We spread out geographically beyond any pro-portion to our population growth. We built a transportation system dominated by cars in a landscape designed for them. We became a decentralized service economy rather than an urban industrial economy. And we became more segregated—by age, by income, by culture, and by race. All of these shifts found physical expression in our development patterns—suburban sprawl and urban decay, diminished natural resources, and lost history.

But just as Edge Cities became the norm, we have outgrown the basic assumptions that encouraged their growth. Land and nature are not boundless. Air quality and congestion limit the monopoly of the car. Middle-class affluence is not universal. The single-family dwelling is not for everyone. In fact, we are no longer a country of nuclear families—only a quarter of American households are now married couples with kids and less than half of them subsist on one income. Since 1950, the per-centage of women working has tripled. The *Leave It to Beaver* version of the American Dream is slipping away.

As this version of the American Dream is aging, we are confronted by other profound changes: the globalization of capital and labor, a growing economic inequality (even in the midst of prosperity), a decaying environment, and a marked erosion of our faith in public institutions, to name just a few. We hear about these changes every day but cannot seem to find the means to organize them into a coherent vision of a personal or cultural future. Many ordinary people respond by withdrawing, cocooning in spe-cial-interest groups and gated communities.

This retreat from a more public life is reinforced by our accelerating tendency to shape communities around special interests rather than around the places we live. "Communities of interest" are the social and economic associations that we form from our particular lifestyle, employment, and social standing. A community of interest is a world filled with people of similar activities, ages, incomes, and values. It is the "gated community" of the mind.

The counterpoint had been the random associations and connections that we devel-oped in our older neighborhoods—places that often fostered a public world that enhanced interaction beyond common interests and like-mindedness. But, as these more diverse "communities of place" became more and more segregated by suburban zoning policies, we lost our day-to-day interaction with a wide range of people—

people not encountered in our communities of interest. A landscape of isolated land uses became a landscape of isolated people.

Even within the more highly segregated developments of today, there is less common ground, less civic space to bring even their homogenous populations together. We leave home in a car and travel to remote workplaces. Without the simple act of walking in our neighborhoods or having something of a common destination, it is little wonder that we know our neighbors less and less. We communicate on the Internet but not on the street.

For some, this is fine: for others, it is debilitating. While the wealthy and mobile can build a complex and rich personal network of associations and opportunities across their region—and in fact the globe—others become more physically, economically, and socially limited. Our two-tiered society and its inequities are magnified by this fundamental difference in the nature of our communities. We are becoming socially more segregated—now by interest, access, and geography as well as income, age, and race.

Part of our inability to come out of our special-interest cocoons and address the massive changes in our time is that our politics operate at the wrong scale. Frustration with centralized public programs has reached a watershed, while local action seems unable to deal with many of our most challenging problems. We are stranded between national solutions too generic, bureaucratic, and large, and local solutions too isolated, anemic, and reactionary. No wonder people become cynical and detached. We live simultaneously at the regional and neighborhood scale but lack a political structure to take advantage of their opportunities.

Many of our policy makers already know that the answers to our most pressing challenges lie in creating regional structures that reduce the sources of economic, social, and environmental stress before they become critical. But, because they operate at the wrong scale, they persist in treating symptoms rather than addressing root causes. As a result, they address inner-city disinvestment with banking regulation and development subsidies, rather than targeting regional economic growth where it is needed most. They control air pollution with tailpipe emissions, fuel consumption with efficiency standards, and congestion with more freeways, rather than making cities and towns that are less automobile dependent. They try to limit lost open space with piecemeal acquisitions, habitat degradation with disconnected reserves, and farmland conversion with tax policies, rather than defining regional forms that are compact and environmentally sound. Too often, they address affordable housing by building isolated blocks of subsidized housing rather than creating mixed-income neighborhoods and implementing regional fair-share housing practices. There is an emerging consensus that these current strategies, though well intentioned and partly successful, are insufficient.

The problems of the Edge City are overwhelming these piecemeal strategies. Its linkages are congested. Its communities are competitive—new suburbs win, first-ring suburbs and cities lose. And its common ground—whether open space, history, or unique cultures—is decaying. The relentless development at the edge around the car is unsustainable, and most of us know it. A new regional order is emerging.

To succeed, this new regional order must reintegrate Edge Cities with old cities and first-ring suburbs. Regional cooperation and coordination is now essential to the success of every town and city. Without a diverse regional transportation network, our neighborhoods and towns easily become isolated pockets surrounded by congestion. Without regional greenbelts, habitat reserves, and farmlands, towns and cities lose their connection to the natural world. Without regional economic strategies, stressed inner suburbs can fall prey to the economic stagnation experienced in many inner-city areas. Without regional access, the truly disadvantaged are cut off from the models and opportunities they need to transform their lives. Without a healthy regional structure and affordable housing, it is increasingly difficult for an area to compete for jobs in a fluid global economy.

Certainly such a framework will require significant social change and progressive economic policies. But much of it has to do with the way we shape our communities: the physical context of our everyday culture. In many unseen ways, urban design and regional form set the physical order of our social structure, the dimensions of our economic needs, and the extent of our environmental impacts. Although it is true that changing the physical form of our communities will not address all our social and ecological challenges, it is also true that economic vitality, social stability, and environmental sustainability cannot be achieved without a coherent and supportive physical framework. Ultimately, it is not one or the other but the way that the two—physical forms and cultural norms—interact.

THE EMERGING REGION, THE MATURING SUBURB, AND THE RENEWED CITY

This book describes three interrelated phenomena: the emergence of regionalism, the maturation of the suburbs, and the revitalization of older urban neighborhoods. Each is a topic unto itself, but each is now critically dependent on the other two. Coherent regional policies can and must support the evolution of the suburbs and the revitalization of the city. They cannot progress without a comprehensive regional vision. Conversely, the physical design of neighborhoods, urban or suburban, can easily negate many regional initiatives. The successful evolution of each—region, suburb, or city—is tied to the others. Taken together, these three trends shape the outlines of a new metropolitan form, what we call the "Regional City."

The first of these three trends, the emergence of regionalism, is clearly upon us. More and more, we live in an aggregation of cities and suburbs: a metropolitan community that forms one economic, cultural, environmental, and civic entity. Out of this aggregation, we would like to paint a picture of a new regional structure. One quite different than the radial vision of Ebenezer Howard's Garden Cities, the modernist's decentralized vision of Greenbelt new towns, or the Edge City standard of existing sprawl. This new regional structure has a more complex form. One that is not focused toward the city or away from it. One that is more like a constellation than a solar system. This emerging region is a layering of networks: networks of communities, networks of open space, networks of economic systems, and networks of cultures. The health of this new region depends on the interconnectedness of these networks, the sophistication of the interfaces, and the vitality of the elements.

The "network" quality of the emerging region is much like the Internet. If the Internet lacked diverse sources of information, if it had congested links, or if it lacked a common language, it would fail. So, too, with regions: to thrive, they need many diverse communities, a variety of connections, and a clearly defined common ground. Although a region's communities range from urban centers to rural villages, each can become at once more centered and more nested into the larger metropolis. Their linkages can combine virtual technology with face-to-face places, just as they can blend the automobile with transit and walking. The region's common ground can be built from its open space systems and its cultural diversity, from its physical history and its economic character.

The emerging region is not dominated by one thing—urbanism, nature, culture, or economy—but by all simultaneously. It cannot be a simple return to central city urbanism or Garden City deconcentration. It is a network of many layers and many types of places. As such, the emerging region has become what the city used to be, the nexus of our culture and the armature of our economy—hence the name Regional City.

At the same time that regionalism is emerging, the suburbs are reaching a transitional stage. Like an adolescent, they have grown so large and uncoordinated that they no longer deliver the qualities that people sought in them. In older suburbs, privacy, mobility, and affordable housing have increasingly been displaced by isolation, grid-lock, and skyrocketing prices. Just as the region emerges as the superstructure of our communities, the suburbs have begun to evolve into something more complex and varied. This evolution involves a kind of infill and redevelopment that overlays the simplistic zoning of the past with richer and more compact choices in housing, transit, and urban form.

This maturation can be largely accomplished through rebuilding the suburb's strip commercial areas, dead mall sites, and obsolete institutional lands—the "Greyfields" of asphalt lining the arterials and highways that divide rather than connect our suburban communities. Inserting urban places—walkable and diverse—into these auto zones may seem radical, but it is, ironically, quite practical. These are the areas most available for change—the zones few care for and none would likely defend. If these Greyfields were transformed, the relentless auto-dominated scale of the suburbs could become punctuated with human-scaled havens, urban outposts in suburbia.

The same urban-design principles that can guide the suburb's maturation can help reshape and repair our most troubled inner-city neighborhoods. In fact, a return to the most basic urban-design ideas—diversity, human scale, and preservation—can begin to heal the damage wrought by the past two generations of urban decay, poor planning, and disinvestment in our cities. Although there are no silver bullets that will pierce the complex layers of urban decay, a regional perspective, good urban design, and comprehensive thinking at the neighborhood scale can begin to correct the structural distress.

Clearly, not all urban ills can be cured quickly or simply. Areas with deep concentrations of poverty and compound social pathologies need enormous change on many levels, as does the society around them. Failing schools, crime, drugs, gangs, fractured families, and joblessness are self-reinforcing realities in many places, both urban and suburban. Many of these problems are the product of larger shifts in our society: the demise of well-paying blue-collar jobs in the cities, the exodus of successful minority families from many ethnic neighborhoods, and the flight of white middle-class residents and jobs to the suburbs. Much of the ghetto culture is due to the collateral effect of these tectonic shifts.

Urban design alone cannot reverse the effects of these fundamental changes; but if it is married to a set of progressive regional policies, revitalization is more than possible. A regional structure that limits sprawl, equalizes tax structures, and redirects development into areas that need it most can fundamentally change the chemistry of many urban neighborhoods. Fair housing policies that balance housing opportunities throughout the region can begin to address the concentrated poverty that suburban sprawl has left in its wake. Acknowledging the transportation needs of the working poor can lead to regional transit systems that provide accessibility from city to suburb as well as the reverse. Facing the problems of urban schools can lead to innovations that expand the meaning and function of education, from preschool and after-school programs through job training and adult education. Understanding that skillful urban design is likely to greatly improve the health of a neighborhood can lead to developments that rediscover the value of urban places.

These three areas are each on the cusp of change: regionalism is a reality about to be born, the suburbs are rapidly maturing, and many inner-city neighborhoods are primed for rebirth. The three are connected by a common design ethic: that communities at the regional or neighborhood scale should have active centers, should respect their history and ecology, and should husband diversity. The challenge is to clarify the connections and shape both neighborhood and region into healthy, sustainable forms—into Regional Cities.

The missing link for many communities has been the loss of some simple and basic urban-design principles. These principles are (as they always have been) to create places that are walkable and human scaled, that are diverse in population and varied in uses, and that are shaped around public spaces that are meaningful and memorable.

Such an urbanism can have many manifestations—from grand and formal city centers to integrated urban neighborhoods, from rural village streets to historic town greens. In all cases, it is not simply density or architecture that constitutes the urbanism, but the coherence of the shared space, the liveliness of the streets, and the complexity of activities. After fifty years of planning that ignored the spaces between projects and buildings, that isolated uses and people, and that elevated the car and marginalized the pedestrian, the simple urbanism of American cities, towns, and villages has a big role to play in the repair of our communities.

This type of urbanism is nothing new. It is an extension of many parallel efforts that have been evolving since Jane Jacobs and William Whyte began their critique of modern architecture and the auto-focused metropolis. Since that time, much has been undertaken to correct Modernism's broad negation of the city. It is now generally accepted that a city's vitality is basically tied to its diversity, pedestrian scale, and civic places. The notion that the auto-oriented suburb is sustainable or even universally desirable is no longer conventional wisdom. Environmental groups have developed to defend the ecosystems and farmlands threatened by sprawl. Inner-city activists have mobilized to revitalize urban neighborhoods and defend them against gentrification. Historic preservation groups have expanded their agendas beyond individual buildings to include whole districts and urban economies. And a multidisciplinary group called the Congress for New Urbanism (see Appendix) has emerged to advocate good urban design at the regional, neighborhood, and building scale.

Combined, these movements now include a diversity of people and professions engaged in a broad range of actions against sprawl and regional inequity. Each has helped to facilitate and support many changes that are part of the making of Regional Cities. Regional plans with complex open-space systems and transit-oriented development have been adopted. Suburban infill projects, replacing strip commercial with mixed-use neighborhoods, are being built throughout the United States. Inner-city housing and neighborhood revitalization has been supported at the federal level by the Department of Housing and Urban Development (HUD) and at the local level by many individual city governments and community groups. Cities, counties, and developers have come to understand and use urbanism in many ways: as the building blocks for "smart growth" at the regional scale, as a way to transform "master-planned communities" into real towns, and as an effective design philosophy for a variety of infill-development sites.

In many ways, then, sprawl and urban disinvestment are under attack, and increasingly losing ground. Many forces are at play in the transformation of the American

Dream and our paradigm of growth. The emerging region, the maturing suburbs, and the revitalization of our older urban neighborhoods are each manifestations of this change. We see the integration of these movements as the foundation of the Regional City.

THE REGIONAL CITY

This book seeks to outline a framework for the Regional City and examine the linkages between the emerging region, evolving suburbs, and renewed inner city. The first part of the book, "The End of Sprawl," lays out the nature and underpinnings of this new metropolitan form. We believe that the Regional City cannot be conceptualized in the traditional terms of city and suburb or even as a collection of political jurisdictions. Rather, the Regional City must be viewed as a cohesive unit—economically, ecologically, and socially—made up of coherent neighborhoods and communities, all of which play a vital role in creating the metropolitan region as a whole.

The second part, "The Architecture of the Regional City," presents our view of the policies and physical design principles required for our metropolitan areas to transform themselves into Regional Cities. The region can and must be shaped through a participatory process to design the physical environment and public policy at both the regional and the neighborhood level. Like the Regional City itself, these designs and policies must be viewed as a cohesive whole, and they require the participation of many players—including the federal government, whose crucial role in determining the nature of regions cannot be overlooked.

The third part, "Regionalism Emerging," documents how many metropolitan areas throughout the United States are transforming themselves into Regional Cities through a combination of physical design and social and economic policies at the regional level. We focus on three cutting-edge Regional Cities—Portland, Seattle, and Salt Lake City. But we also consider the difficulties of implementing policies at a regional scale in very large metropolitan regions, and we pay particular attention to the potential role of state government in certain areas, including Florida, Maryland, and Minnesota.

The final part, "Renewing the Region's Communities," focuses on the two neighborhood-scaled phenomena that are shaping metropolitan regions at the local level—the maturation of sprawling suburbs and the renewal of urban neighborhoods. Although we deal with these two trends separately, they are really intertwined with each other and with regional efforts in general. Maturing suburbs and renewed urban neighborhoods need regional policies that deal with large-scale social and economic trends as well as physical planning that reasserts the lost art of urban design.

SPRAWL AND INEQUITY

Throughout this book, we will frequently speak of the twin problems of sprawl and inequity. We do so because we believe that these problems are related to one another, and both emerge from the destructive metropolitan patterns that have shaped our nation for the past half-century. On a regional level, sprawl exacerbates inequity, and growing inequity, in turn, begets more sprawl. We believe that neither problem can be effectively dealt with if the two problems are not addressed together. A fundamental tenet of the Regional City is the pursuit of diversity, both at the regional and at the neighborhood level, in a way that is meant to combat inequity as well as sprawl.

Having stated our belief that sprawl and inequity are twin problems, it is important for us to add that, in our view, inequity is a much more intractable problem than sprawl. Sprawl is a recent phenomenon and a solvable problem. As we and many others have pointed out, we know what causes sprawl (low densities, segregation of uses, auto orientation) and we know how to attack them. Inequity, on the other hand, is an eternal problem. It existed long before sprawl, in small towns, in rural areas, and in industrial cities. It is caused not only by the physical environment, but also by a whole range of common human feelings such as greed, elitism, and racism.

Greater minds than ours have sought unsuccessfully to solve the problem of inequity in our society, and we do not pretend that our ideas for the Regional City will eradicate it. However, we do believe that inequity in the contemporary American condition needs to be attacked along with sprawl and its complement, urban disinvestment, and that both need to be addressed at the level of the region and the neighborhood. For two generations, Americans have sought to eradicate urban decay and the problems created by growing concentrations of poverty in the inner city. But this effort has been largely unsuccessful—in part because it has attacked inequity as a discrete problem of the city, without recognizing how metropolitan growth patterns increased the urban decay and concentration of poverty in the first place. Combating sprawl will not end inequity, but an end to inequity cannot be achieved without addressing sprawl.

We believe that the United States is in a transition to a new paradigm of growth. Sprawl's tendency to fracture local communities, empty our cities, and consume the natural and agrarian landscape is coming to an end. The suburban divide, that version of the American Dream that segregated our culture into low-density winners and urban losers, is breaking down. Increasingly, the middle class and underclass have problems in common—dysfunctional transportation systems, poor education, crime, pollution, lack of open space, and decaying neighborhoods—to which there can be common solutions. This is the real power of the Regional City: it can unify now disconnected interest groups by addressing their problems with shared strategies. The elements of the Regional City—transit, affordable housing fairly distributed, environmental preserves, walkable communities, urban reinvestments, and infill development—now benefit a growing cross section of our population and represent a powerful new political coalition.

This book is an attempt to lay out the processes, policies, and designs that can give shape and identity to these new strategies—to describe the emerging metropolitan network of the Regional City and its complement, the simple urbanism of walkable neighborhoods and diverse communities. The Regional City is built by intensifying places and intensifying connections—making them more complex, inclusive, and varied. It is not a choice between city and suburb, between virtual communities and physical places, between history and future, or between communities of interest or communities of place. At its best, it creates places in which we can live in all simultaneously, which is what we all seek to do anyway.

PART ONE:
THE END OF SPRAWL

Most Americans today do not live in towns—or even in cities—in the traditional sense that we think of those terms. Instead, most of us are citizens of a region—a large and multifaceted metropolitan area encompassing hundreds of places that we would traditionally think of as distinct and separate "communities."

CHAPTER 1:

LIVING IN THE REGIONAL WORLD

Only a century ago, the archetypal American community was a small city—often a factory town or a farm market town—so self-contained that its residents rarely had to leave its boundaries to obtain their daily needs. So small was Gopher Prairie, the locale of Sinclair Lewis's famous 1920 novel, *Main Street,* that in one thirty-two-minute walk his protagonist Carol Kennicott "had completely covered the town, east and west, north and south." Beyond Gopher Prairie's borders, as Carol quickly discovered, was nothing but "the grasping prairie on every side."

Almost a century later, Carol Kennicott could walk all day and probably never find the prairie. Today, more than half of all Americans live in metropolitan areas of a million people or more. Fully a third of the people in the country—approximately 90 million in all—live in the twenty or so largest metropolitan areas, according to the latest census figures. The urban space regularly traversed by the typical American is not really a "community" at all, but rather a series of connected urban and suburban districts that often stretch across a vast geographical space. Very few people in our country today can cover the entirety of their daily travels in a five- or ten-minute walk.

In other words, most Americans today do not live in towns—or even in cities—in the traditional sense that we think of those terms. Instead, most of us are citizens of a region—a large and multifaceted metropolitan area encompassing hundreds of places that we would traditionally think of as distinct and separate "communities."

Of course, most of us do not think of ourselves as living in a region. Strolling in our neighborhood or visiting our local shopping center, we still tend to think of ourselves as inhabitants of Gopher Prairie. But the patterns of our daily existence belie a different reality. Most of us commute from one metropolitan town to another for work, for shopping, and for many other daily activities. The businesses for which we work are typically bound up in a series of economic relationships with vendors and customers that are concentrated on a regional or metropolitan scale.

- *Mobility:* a transportation plan

- *Workforce:* a plan to focus on workforce education to improve the region's competitiveness

- *Governance:* a series of proposals to improve regional governance and coordination among the hundreds of governmental units within the region

A regional plan covering 13,000 square miles is necessarily broad in scope, but *A Region at Risk* made a significant effort to frame the issues in terms of regional design. In particular, the Greensward and Centers concepts provided a physical framework for the region's future growth.

The Greensward plan (which adopted the term used by Frederick Law Olmsted and Calvert Vaux in describing their design for Central Park) identifies eleven key landscape-level ecosystems and open-space areas, totaling 2.5 million acres, that are to serve as the backbone of a "regional reserve" system. They include such important areas as the Catskill Mountains, the Atlantic seashore, the Long Island Pine Barrens, and the highlands to the north and west of New York City through which the Appalachian Trail meanders.

The Centers plan reflects the undeniable fact that, despite the overwhelming presence of Manhattan, metropolitan New York is a multicentered region—a metropolitan constellation with many strong and important downtowns. Just as the Greensward plan identifies eleven landscapes in need of protection, the Centers plan identifies eleven regional downtowns outside of Manhattan and Brooklyn—including Newark and Trenton in New Jersey, New Haven and Bridgeport in Connecticut, and Mineola and Hicksville on Long Island—and calls for heavy investment in these areas.

The Mobility plan builds on the Centers concept by proposing the so-called Rx system, or Regional Express Rail system, which will fill existing gaps in the regional system and make traveling throughout the entire New York region by rail a much more convenient proposition.

Although it has been only a few years since *A Region at Risk* was issued, it is already clear that the plan has had a major effect on the New York region in certain ways. The Greensward plan has proved to be a focal point for many regional efforts at open-space preservation, including the acquisition of the 15,800-acre Sterling Forest property in Orange County, New York, and the commitment of New Jersey Governor Christie

Todd Whitman to spend $1 billion to ensure that 40 percent of the state's land is permanently protected. Similarly, the Rx transportation plan has stimulated new action on important but long-stalled transportation projects throughout the region, such as the Second Avenue subway in Manhattan and rail links to Newark and Kennedy airports. A number of new civic coalitions have emerged around specific recommendations in the plan, including, for example, a business–civic–environmental coalition to examine transportation issues along the I-95 corridor in Connecticut.

At the same time, the experience of implementing *A Region at Risk* shows how difficult it can be to deal with the entire panoply of physical-design issues at the level of the superregion. Though it is blessed with many handsome maps of the region, as well as important design ideas for how to handle increased development in the region's centers, *A Region at Risk* is not really a physical plan for the design of the entire region. And it may not be possible to create such a plan for an enormous geographical area such as metropolitan New York. *A Region at Risk* seems to reveal that, in superregions, it may be possible to stimulate compelling physical plans for subregions, as has been the case in New Jersey, but this accomplishment may come at the risk of losing the regionwide perspective, as has also been the case in New Jersey.

In assessing the *Region at Risk* experience, the RPA's executive director, Robert Yaro, has stressed the importance of what he calls "The Three T's" ("Things Take Time") and "The Three P's" (Persistence, Patience, and Perseverance). For example, the acquisition of Sterling Forest—a major component in shaping the physical form of the region—was first proposed in the 1929 Regional Plan, but it wasn't actually accomplished for seventy years. The New York experience suggests that even though "things take time," a broad regional framework allows big-picture discussion of the physical framework of a metropolitan area.

CHICAGO METROPOLIS 2020

Like New York, Chicago is a mature metropolis with a distinguished planning history that has suffered in recent years from significant inner-city decline and suburban sprawl. But, as a Regional City, Chicago presents a somewhat different challenge than New York.

Similar to New York, Chicago has had a stagnant population and an uneven economy in recent decades. But unlike New York, economic growth in Chicago is driven by one strong downtown—the Loop—and a few other large job centers, such as the area surrounding O'Hare Airport, meaning that many parts of the region have been left behind economically. Metropolitan Chicago remains extremely segregated by race— the term *hypersegregation* is often used in reference to Chicago—and the region is extremely fragmented politically.

Although Chicago has often been a leader in urban design, it does not have the same rich history of regional visioning that the Regional Plan Association has provided to New York. It's true that Daniel Burnham's 1909 plan for the city of Chicago—prepared for a business group, the Commercial Club of Chicago—remains one of the finest documents of the City Beautiful era. By providing for a system of parks and parkways, especially along Lake Michigan, it brought urbane grace and beauty to a city where such amenities had been conspicuously lacking. Despite this achievement, however, metropolitan Chicago subsequently developed a uniquely fragmented urban structure that reinforced regional imbalances and worked against regional cooperation.

Traditionally, the region has been sharply divided between the city of Chicago— urban, high density, and heavily black—and some 260 suburban municipalities, mostly white with lower densities. Segregation and inequity are deeply embedded within this regional structure. Almost 1.5 million African Americans live in metropolitan Chicago, yet they remain concentrated in highly segregated neighborhoods. Three-quarters of the black population lives inside the Chicago city limits, and most of those residents live in neighborhoods that are almost entirely African American.

At the same time, classic sprawl developed throughout the region. Between 1970 and 1990, metropolitan Chicago's population barely grew at all, yet the urbanized area increased by approximately 35 percent. The reason is simple: a large part of the region's population (especially white middle-class and upper-middle-class residents) fled to the metropolitan fringe. Chicago and the older close-in suburbs lost some 800,000 residents, whereas the outer-ring suburbs, such as Bolingbrook and Naperville, added nearly a million people. The resulting inequity was stark; the per capita income disparity between the richest and the poorest jurisdictions in the Chicago region doubled in the 1980s.

Although the black population has remained heavily concentrated inside the city limits of Chicago, other minority groups—predominantly Latinos—have begun to move into older, inner-ring suburbs in large numbers. At the same time, these older suburbs—which have traditionally viewed themselves as nonurban because they wanted to separate themselves from Chicago—have begun to face typical problems of land-poor communities. Myron Orfield found that, by the 1990s, Chicago had fractured into at least five types of communities sharply divided by fiscal capacity. The city of Chicago had an average tax base per household of $83,000—only two-thirds of the region's average of $127,000. The inner suburbs and the communities on the metropolitan fringe also had low tax bases—approximately $100,000 per household. The only areas that exceeded the region's average tax base per household were the older affluent suburbs in the northwestern part of the region, including such communities as Shaumberg, adjacent to O'Hare Airport, and the rapidly growing suburban areas south of the city.

Both sprawl and inequity are well-known problems in the Chicago area. But, in the 1990s, local civic leaders and citizen activists began to understand the connection between the two for the first time—largely because the region's problems were getting worse. Chicago's population was increasing faster than it had in decades, thanks in large part to a rapid rise in the Latino population. Meanwhile, low-density growth in the outer-ring suburbs appeared likely to continue, mostly for the benefit of the white population. In the 1990s, a whole range of groups—business groups, grassroots organizations, and government agencies—began taking steps to address the twin problems of sprawl and inequity in Chicago.

In 1995, a citizen coalition led by the Center for Neighborhood Technology produced a Citizen Transportation Plan that called for regional tax-base sharing and emphasis on infill development and transit-oriented transportation investments. In 1998, the regional planning agency, the Northeast Illinois Planning Commission (NIPC), made a similar series of recommendations. But perhaps the biggest push toward the Regional City in Chicago came when the Commercial Club—the same group of business leaders that sponsored the Burnham Plan in 1909—undertook a regional assessment similar to New York's Regional Plan Association's *A Region at Risk*.

Just as the 1909 plan was spearheaded by Daniel Burnham, the Commercial Club's report was spearheaded by another civic leader—Elmer Johnson, a Chicago attorney (and now president of the Aspen Institute in Washington, D.C.) A former executive vice president of General Motors, Johnson is, ironically, a passionate advocate of broader transportation alternatives. His prestige gave the Commercial Club effort a gravity that other regional planning efforts in Chicago simply didn't have.

Chicago Metropolis 2020 is different from *A Region at Risk* in that it is not especially focused on large-scale elements of physical design for the region. *Chicago Metropolis 2020* does an excellent job of identifying problems associated with geographical disparity and inequity and, most important, connecting the need for better regional policies on social and economic issues to the need for better physical design of the region as a whole. In particular, the plan highlights the need for reform in housing, education, and tax equity—three elements described in the preceding section as being at the core of regional equity issues.

On education, *Chicago Metropolis 2020* calls for both greater tax equity and more school choice. For decades, Chicago's property-taxation system—which provides the basis for school funding—has been unusually arcane, with local governments assessing and taxing property by using a bewildering array of percentages and fractions. At the same time, the inequity in local property-taxation systems has led to a vast gap within the region. In 1990, the richest 10 percent of school districts had thirteen times the tax base of the poorest 10 percent. Partly as a result of such statistics, the state legislature has now established a per pupil "floor" for school funding, but *Chicago Metropolis 2020* calls for a broader base of funding for schools, including the possibility of a statewide system of property-tax sharing. *Chicago Metropolis 2020* also recognizes the need for greater parental control of schools and greater school choice, at least among public schools.

Fair housing is probably at the core of the Chicago dilemma. As the preceding statistics suggest, few metropolitan regions have been as deeply harmed by housing discrimination as Chicago. *Chicago Metropolis 2020* identifies a series of fair-housing policies already underway in Chicago—as well as many others than could be implemented—and divides these strategies into "supply side" and "demand side" approaches. Under supply-side approaches, the plan calls for continued reform of public housing, which in Chicago has included razing unsuccessful high-rise "projects" and replacing them with smaller-scale, mixed-income projects such as the HOPE VI projects described in Part Four. Under demand-side strategies, the plan highlights the Gautreaux program described in Chapter 4 and calls for an expansion of housing vouchers to permit more mobility among lower-income families. The plan proposes a much-expanded Section 8 voucher program to facilitate more Gautreaux-style efforts.

These proposed strategies are the very essence of the Regional City concept. By applying both supply-side and demand-side approaches, *Chicago Metropolis 2020* seeks to create a better balance of housing and incomes throughout the entire region. Although the plan contains many other proposals, including a link between land-use and transportation planning and the creation of a regional system of greenways, these proposals are designed to reinforce a regional solution to Chicago's most basic problem, the income disparity and hypersegregation. Now, *Chicago Metropolis 2020* has a group working to implement the ideas contained in the plan, under the leadership of George Ranney, an attorney and innovative developer.

As with the Regional Plan Association, the role of Chicago Metropolis 2020 in implementing the ideas in the plan has been to serve as catalyst and cajoler. Among other things, Metropolis's early achievements included bringing business executives together with social-service agencies to discuss how best to deal with early childhood education in the region and to reorganize the region's fragmented approach to regional transportation. Previously, several regional transportation agencies divided the pie on the basis of political clout; now, under a new agreement, they will work together and allocate more resources to regional planning.

Metropolis and other groups have not yet made much of a dent in the hypersegregation program, which is both the most difficult and the most intractable problem in metropolitan Chicago. A follow-up report on rental housing, funded by a variety of agencies, documented the tight rental housing market in Chicago and called for an expanded voucher program.

The Regional City effort in Chicago is still young, and it will probably take many years for it to mature. It is clear that both the physical-design approaches and the social-economic policies discussed earlier will be required in strong combination with one another to transform Chicago into a true Regional City. There is little question that the business community—a critical element in regional success—is poised to play a critical role in using Regional-City concepts to attack Chicago's most fundamental problems.

THE SAN FRANCISCO BAY AREA

Other than New York, there is probably no metropolis in the United States with a longer tradition of regional planning—and a stronger sense of regional identity—than the San Francisco Bay area. Part of this strong sense of identity is clearly due to topography. The Bay Area is traditionally defined as including the nine counties that touch the San Francisco Bay—the most important natural estuary on the West Coast and the largest and most distinctive natural feature in the entire region. Part of it, too, is the fact that the Bay Area was a pioneer in fostering the notion among citizen groups, business leaders, and elected officials that they must think of themselves as a Regional City. Citizen activism on planning issues dates back to the 1950s, and, from the beginning, citizen groups took a regional approach, especially on open space and transportation matters.

Far more than that of New York or Chicago, however, the experience of regionalism in the Bay Area must be viewed as a decentralized and incremental effort—an accumulation of plans, ideas, implementation strategies, and community activism that has built up over a period of four decades to shape the Bay Area as a Regional City. This singular experience, which stands in contrast with most other regionalism efforts throughout the country, yields several important lessons—both for regionalism generally and for regional efforts in the superregions specifically.

First, dedicated action on the part of regional citizen and business groups has provided measurable results for the entire region. Second, it has been very difficult to bring government agencies, especially local government agencies, together to work on regional problems—in large part because the state government has failed to provide a strong growth-management framework. Third, citizen groups and local government agencies have worked together well at the subregional level, producing effective designs for such subregions as the South Bay (Silicon Valley) and the North Bay (the beautiful area of Marin County and the Napa and Sonoma Valleys). And, finally, all the successes and failures of the past forty years have not dampened the appetite of both citizen activists and business leaders for a stronger effort at the level of the entire region.

Other than the bay itself, what distinguishes the Bay Area—and, indeed, makes it a model for the twenty-first-century metropolitan region—is the fact that it is not dominated by only one central city. Although world-famous, San Francisco is merely the second-largest city in the region (behind San Jose, the largest city), and it is one of three cities (Oakland being the third) that can legitimately lay claim to being a "central city." No one city contains more than about 13 percent of the region's population of more than six million people. But the three central cities together account for about a third of the region's population.

Perhaps for this reason, both citizen activism and government action to deal with issues on a regional scale date back to the 1950s, when postwar suburban sprawl was cutting into the hillsides south of San Francisco, the rich agricultural land around San Jose, and other such locations. Between the late 1950s and the early 1970s, citizen groups such as People for Open Space (now Greenbelt Alliance) and others agitated for regional action on such issues as preserving open space, and providing public-transit alternatives to then-common freeway projects. As a result, many regional government agencies were organized by local officials or created by the state government. The East Bay Regional Park District and the Midpeninsula Regional Open Space District created a magnificent open-space system in the eastern and southern parts of the region. The Bay Conservation and Development Commission reversed the alarming trend of "filling in" San Francisco Bay. The Bay Area Rapid Transit District was created to build BART, the first regional rail passenger system constructed anywhere in the United States since the 1920s. The Association of Bay Area Governments (ABAG)—the Bay Area's council of governments (COG)—was created earlier than almost any other COG in the United States and quickly began to advocate a city-centered regional plan that would focus new growth in existing urban areas.

As more than one city planning historian has pointed out, this list is far more extensive than almost any other region in the United States has accomplished, during this or any other era. Yet, despite these accomplishments, the Bay Area has not succeeded in fully shaping a Regional City. And the reasons are instructive. Perhaps most important is the fact that, for some twenty years, the Bay Area's efforts at regionalism got bogged down in a seemingly endless debate over what form a regional government should take. The debate was similar in many parts of the country, especially in the 1960s and 1970s. But in the Bay Area it was especially intense. A proposal to make ABAG a true regional government—with power over local authority—fell apart in the 1960s. Then, in the 1980s, a blue-ribbon commission proposed a new regional structure, but it focused on a merger of existing bureaucracies, including ABAG and the regional transportation and air-quality agencies. By focusing on rearranging bureaucrats rather than on regional visioning, the Bay Vision 2020 effort fell apart as well.

In the absence of either a regional vision or a true regional government, the Bay Area developed what might be called an "ad hoc regionalism." Citizen groups such as Greenbelt Alliance took it on themselves to draw up their own regional strategies and try to implement them piece by piece. Greenbelt, for example, devised its own plan to preserve open space by containing urban growth and focusing development on existing urban centers. Then the organization implemented its strategy by running initiative campaigns in individual cities throughout the Bay Area—almost all of them successful—to create greenlines around those cities.

At the same time, local governments worked with citizen and business groups to draft visions and implementation strategies at the subregional level. Largely thanks to the leadership of the computer industry, Silicon Valley has made enormous strides in the past decade in viewing itself as a true Regional City. The local governments in the area—including Santa Clara County and the City of San Jose, by far the two largest jurisdictions—have agreed on a Greenline urban growth boundary. San Jose and several other communities have greatly intensified their efforts to allow denser housing in existing neighborhoods. And, in an effort to free up more land for housing, many of the Silicon Valley cities have also jointly agreed to rezone industrial land for residential use. They have also constructed a new light rail, which complements a massive effort to urbanize the downtown of San Jose. In large part, these efforts have been successful because, in superregions such as the Bay Area, the subregion is a manageable unit, approximately the same size as Seattle or Salt Lake City.

All these efforts are commendable, and they reinforce the Bay Area's longstanding reputation as a leader in innovative regional efforts. But they also reveal the difficulties in trying to shape a Regional City in an ad hoc way. Citizen groups may pursue partial solutions or subregional cooperation may lead to progress, but the overall growth of the region as a whole is rarely addressed in a comprehensive way. As a result, local and subregional goals are often met, but the region as a whole has become more and more imbalanced. During the Silicon Valley Internet boom of the 1990s, for example, nine jobs were created in Santa Clara County for every house constructed. As the Silicon Valley boom stimulated housing construction in other parts of the Bay Area, many communities—including some that had already adopted greenlines—imposed further growth controls to restrict housing. These local actions created a "domino effect" that pushed needed affordable housing over the mountains into the Central Valley.

These new problems have created the latest additions to the Bay Area's ad hoc regionalism; recently, local officials in the Bay Area and Central Valley have together created an organization (the Inter-Regional Partnership) to deal with joint issues. But all these efforts, commendable though they may be, seek to deal with problems created by the fact that the region has not successfully grappled with the question of how to organize regional growth in physical terms. Despite forty years of activism by local governments, businesses, and citizen groups, the Bay Area still has not dealt head-on with the choices that the region must make in comprehensive and physical terms, as Envision Utah did for Salt Lake City.

In large part, these ongoing problems with transforming the Bay Area into a true Regional City have emerged from the fact that California has not provided strong state leadership for regional planning or regional visioning. To be sure, California has many, many laws dealing with land-use planning, transportation, and environmental protection. Unlike such states as Oregon, Washington, Florida, and Maryland, however, California has never taken a leadership role in setting strong statewide principles and policies for metropolitan growth. In the absence of a statewide framework, local governments—and even subregional coalitions—have been able to pursue their own objectives without considering the overall regional effects of their actions. (This lack of state leadership has also hindered regionalism efforts in the Los Angeles area, which has a much more troubled history of dealing with regional planning issues.)

Fortunately, many of the Bay Area's leading businesses and citizen leaders still recognize the need for this kind of full-scale regional design discussion. Recently, a broad coalition of leaders, including business and government leaders, environmentalists, and developers, signed on to a proposed "Compact for a Sustainable Bay Area."

In signing the compact, these regional leaders—called together by the Bay Area Council, a regional business group of long-standing credibility—committed themselves to ten regional principles. These included such goals as pursuing "a diversified, sustainable, and competitive economy," accommodating sufficient housing, focusing on preserving and revitalizing neighborhoods, and creating more cooperation among competing local governments.

The Compact for a Sustainable Bay Area will now serve as the basis for a regional design "visioning" process not unlike the one in Salt Lake City—setting the stage for the possibility of real progress in regional design in the Bay Area at last. Despite the Bay Area's historic inability to deal with regional issues in a comprehensive, design-oriented fashion, the Sustainable Bay Area effort is proof that the Bay Area superregion still holds the potential to be transformed into a true Regional City.

CHAPTER 8:

STATE-LED REGIONALISM:
FLORIDA, MARYLAND, & MINNESOTA

Ever since Oregon's growth-management law was passed in 1973, many planning and design leaders have argued that the only way to deal with matters of regional growth and design is through state legislation. Because regional governments are so often weak and toothless, the argument goes, only the state government has the political clout to impose regional goals and hold local governments accountable for achieving them. There is no question that, in many cases, ironclad state goals are required as part of the framework for the Regional City. Neither Portland nor Seattle would have succeeded in its metropolitan growth strategies without state laws. And New Jersey would not have embarked on an ambitious fair-housing effort were it not for state requirements—first from the courts and later from the legislature. By the same token, there is little question that the San Francisco Bay area would have had more success over the years in pursuing a regional strategy if such efforts had been supported by strong and clear state policies.

However, the mere existence of a set of laws and policies at the state level does not, by itself, ensure that an effort to shape a Regional City will succeed. The nature and character of those state laws and policies matter a great deal as well. And the recent experience of what we call "state-led regionalism" suggests that the bureaucratic, regulatory approaches that states have traditionally adopted cannot by themselves be effective. They must be supported by a whole panoply of affirmative efforts to promote the concept of the Regional City. In particular, they cannot succeed without a design concept that translates the policies and regulations into a physical vision of what the region should look like. This chapter focuses on three states—Florida, Maryland, and Minnesota—whose very different experiences in state-led regionalism all point to this same lesson.

FLORIDA

With more than fifteen million people, Florida is the largest state in the nation with a comprehensive statewide growth-management law. Yet fifteen years of experience under the Growth Management Act has not really led to a greater sense of regionalism in Florida's leading metropolitan areas. For this reason, the Florida experience is instructive in explaining what state legislation can and cannot do in helping to design the Regional City.

The 1985 growth-management law established a few important statewide growth goals, such as encouraging compact urban development, keeping growth away from Florida's fragile coasts, and requiring that infrastructure be put in place to accommodate all new development. It also required coordinated state approval of all local plans in each county. But, at its core, the Florida law was not really focused on the goals of the Regional City as we have outlined them in this book—to overcome sprawl and inequity. Rather, the law as it was written in 1985 focused mostly on managing future urban expansion and, especially, on ensuring that public infrastructure was adequate to accommodate urban growth.

The most important provision of the Florida law was a policy that came to be known as "concurrency"—a requirement that local governments identify funding sources and a construction schedule for all roads, sewers, and other public infrastructure required to accommodate new development. Concurrency is an important goal, and, by requiring a cost analysis for new infrastructure, the concurrency requirement lowered infrastructure costs that led, in many cases, to more compact development. But the law did not directly address the physical form of metropolitan growth—a deficiency that became all too apparent as sprawl became more important in the 1990s.

As one statewide commission reviewing the Growth Management Act recently concluded, concurrency "has been implemented almost exclusively as 'motor vehicle concurrency.'" As with federal transportation policy, the analytical tools used in analyzing concurrency were focused almost entirely on highways, automobiles, and traditional measurements such as "levels of service" without considering land-use alternatives, standards of community design, and public transit. Indeed, public-transit facilities themselves were subject to the state's concurrency requirements.

The result was more sprawl. With a system of analysis geared only toward cars, growth was encouraged on the metropolitan fringe (where highway capacity was available) and often prohibited in existing urban areas (where highway capacity was limited). In many cases, this situation also increased congestion and lengthened commutes, because residents living in new subdivisions on the metropolitan fringe often commuted to existing urban areas (where new development was prohibited) to get to their jobs.

The concurrency problem has been partly rectified by a series of incremental legislative changes in the past decade. The state now permits urban areas to create "concurrency exception areas," where infill development should be encouraged, and permits local governments to designate "infill and redevelopment" areas, where a significant deviation from concurrency standards is permitted.

But, even after fifteen years of amendments, the Florida situation still suffers from a major flaw: the law does not encourage local governments to stop competing with one another and start working together from a regional perspective. This is especially true in metropolitan areas that consist of more than one county, as do all three of the state's large metropolitan areas (Miami, Orlando, and Tampa–St. Petersburg).

With the exception of large projects (known as Developments of Regional Impact, or DRI), the Growth Management Act creates little regional perspective. Indeed, it bypasses the regional perspective by creating a direct relationship between the state government and the local governments. Although the state's Department of Community Affairs is obligated to review a county's plan and the plans of all cities in that county at the same time, it still does not deal with large metropolitan areas in their entirety.

In some parts of the state, a regional boundary was established—but often at the county level, which was inadequate. For example, Orange County (where Orlando is located) created an Urban Service Area boundary. But developers responded by simply leaping over the county line into adjacent counties, which were more than happy to accept new growth.

These large "leapfrog" projects were subject to the regional DRI process, but they often won approval anyway if they were able to "capture" most of their traffic internally and therefore had a minimal impact on the surrounding highway system. Ironically, the state's growth-management law often favored New Urbanist designs for these noncontiguous "new towns." The New Urbanist plans were thoughtfully designed and could prove, at least in theory, that they would have minimal effect on the traffic of surrounding towns and highways. But this system of permitting new towns did little to address overall metropolitan sprawl. In fact, it perpetuated the myth that New Urbanism was promoting nothing more than a somewhat different kind of sprawl.

In short, the lack of a metropolitan perspective has greatly harmed Florida's efforts to manage growth. The result is great variation in the way in which different metropolitan regions deal with growth. As stated earlier, jurisdictions in the Orlando area—and other metropolitan areas that still perceive themselves to be land rich—can comply with the requirements of the Growth Management Act without working together to combat sprawl or inequity. In contrast, in South Florida (Miami), urban sprawl has pushed metropolitan growth to the edge of the Everglades. The region cannot expand outward geographically without more environmental destruction of the Everglades, which has become a major—and extremely expensive—environmental priority for both the state and the federal governments in the 1990s.

For this reason, many local governments in South Florida were receptive to the state's efforts to promote sustainable communities, including the Eastward Ho! initiative, which took direct aim at protecting the environment, curbing suburban sprawl, and revitalizing urban neighborhoods as part of an integrated package. Rather than focusing on the bureaucratic requirements of infrastructure adequacy, Eastward Ho! focused on reshaping the entire South Florida metropolis physically so as to transform it into a Regional City. It did so by cleaning up brownfields, redeveloping existing neighborhoods, creating regional urban boundaries, and connecting urban-growth policy in South Florida to efforts to restore the Everglades.

Under Governor Jeb Bush, the state has cut back support for the Eastward Ho! initiative, and it is unclear whether the local governments in South Florida will "step up to the plate" to continue the area's movement toward a Regional City. But the lesson of Florida is clear: policy-based efforts to manage growth that do not focus on regional form and inequity will likely fail because of local government competition and unintended consequences that may lead to more sprawl, not less. Sprawl is not a problem that can be overcome simply by bureaucratic processes; rather, it must be addressed through a conscious effort of regional and neighborhood design that capitalizes on the potential of existing urban and suburban neighborhoods and districts.

MARYLAND

Whereas the Florida Growth Management Act deals largely with bureaucratic processes, the Maryland Smart Growth program focuses almost entirely on the question of regional form. Although it is still in its infancy (the law was passed in 1997), the Smart Growth program is a good example of how innovative state policies can support local efforts to overcome sprawl and can do so by using public investment, rather than state regulation, as the vehicle.

When Parris Glendening was elected governor in 1994, he decided to make anti-sprawl policy a centerpiece of his campaign. Not unlike South Florida, Maryland is a region of great natural beauty and agricultural productivity that is deeply afflicted by problems of sprawl and inequity at the metropolitan level. Baltimore and Washington are among the strongest and most successful metropolitan regions in the United States—in many ways they constitute one prosperous superregion—but their central cities are mostly African American and extremely poor.

Determining to protect rural areas and stimulate investment in existing urban areas, Glendening, a former college professor and local government official, coined the term "Smart Growth" and proposed a series of state policy changes that would direct new growth away from agricultural land and toward urban neighborhoods in need of investment.

In most other states, beginning with Oregon, the effort to end sprawl and transform metropolitan areas had rested on heavy regulation. But, in Maryland, Glendening did not have the luxury of creating regulatory restrictions on urban growth. The property-rights movement had won many successes in court, giving landowners more power and making it more difficult—both legally and politically—for governments to create more regulation.

Glendening chose a different tack. He attempted to influence growth patterns by directing state investment into specific locations. As he later put it, "We decided to use our (state) budget as a $15 billion incentive for Smart Growth. And we have begun to use our tax laws as a disincentive to sprawl." He used the term *Smart Growth* largely for marketing purposes, believing that no political opponent would dare come out in favor of *Dumb Growth*.

The "Smart Growth and Neighborhood Conservation program," passed in 1997, has two major components. Both reallocate existing state funds to deal with the twin problems of sprawl and inequity. The first major component identifies Priority Funding Areas throughout the state and channels most state infrastructure money into those areas. Existing municipalities, for example, are automatically designated as Priority Funding Areas under the state law, as are areas inside the Washington and Baltimore beltways, enterprise zones, and state-designated revitalization areas. Some greenfield areas may also be designated as Priority Funding Areas, as long as they have a housing density of at least 3.5 units per acre—not enough density to support transit but enough to discourage large-lot "rural" subdivisions.

The second major component, known as the Rural Legacy program, channels the state's land-acquisition funds into designated conservation areas. Maryland already had one of the oldest and most generously funded land-conservation programs in the nation. The Smart Growth program ensured that this money was spent more strategically to protect key agricultural land, curb suburban sprawl, and direct growth into existing urban areas.

Maryland's Smart Growth law is far from perfect. The lack of regulatory teeth clearly makes it difficult for the state to achieve its goals. In addition, the counties are permitted to designate some of their own "Smart Growth" priority funding areas. They and have not always done a conscientious job, at least according to one report from 1000 Friends of Maryland, a watchdog group. But even short of perfection, the Maryland Smart Growth effort has already paid off.

Using Smart Growth criteria, Glendening canceled the construction of all highway bypasses in the state. (Meanwhile, the Maryland suburbs of Washington, D.C., are connected to Washington's superior regional subway system, and Baltimore is building a light-rail system.) More than 80 percent of all state school construction money is now being spent in existing urban areas, compared with only 42 percent at the time that he took office. And the state recently reported that in 1999, for the first time ever, more land was conserved as a result of the state's efforts than was consumed by new urban growth. In a very short time, the Smart Growth approach has allowed both Baltimore and the Maryland suburbs of Washington, D.C., to take an entirely new approach to dealing with metropolitan growth, one that is likely to reduce regional sprawl and inequity in the years ahead.

MINNESOTA

For almost thirty years, advocates of regional planning throughout the United States have pointed to the Twin Cities—the Minneapolis–St. Paul metropolitan region in Minnesota—as a shining example of regional cooperation designed to promote regional equity. In large part, however, this reputation is based on one regional policy: the regional tax-sharing policy, which redistributes of some of the growth in property taxes from tax-rich jurisdictions to tax-poor jurisdictions. This policy is an important national precedent, and it has done a great deal to bring more tax equity to the region. But, as the political and civic leaders of the Twin Cities have lately begun to recognize, neither this single policy nor the region's long and impressive history of regional cooperation—impressive, at least, by American standards—has been sufficient to stem the tide of sprawl and inequity. A more comprehensive and design-conscious vision is required as well.

With approximately 2.5 million people, the Twin Cities region is on the high end of the midsized metropolitan regions that include Seattle, Portland, and Salt Lake City. Unlike most other Midwestern metropolises, the Twin Cities region is still experiencing considerable population growth and economic expansion. The population of the region has increased by more than 25 percent since 1980. Jobs have increased by 20 percent in just the past decade. And, whereas growth in the two central cities and older suburbs was stagnant, the population increased dramatically in newer, low-density suburbs such as Maple Grove, a small community located northwest of Minneapolis that became a focal point for debate about density, growth, and regionalism in the 1990s.

Like the San Francisco Bay area, the Twin Cities got into the business of regionalism early in the game—in large part because of the very practical need to better coordinate regional sewage problems. The Metropolitan Council, a regional agency covering seven counties, was established in 1967. Unlike the Association of Bay Area Governments and other regional agencies, however, the Met Council is not a loose and voluntary organization of local governments. Rather, it is a state-chartered entity, financed independently by a small part of the property tax, with a governing board appointed partly at the state level and charged with making important decisions about regional facilities such as airports. This state-led regionalism is an important distinction from the ad hoc regionalism of the Bay Area. Among other things, the Met Council was charged with creating and maintaining a Metropolitan Urban Service Area, or MUSA—an urban services line beyond which urban development was not to be permitted. Like other similar laws elsewhere, the MUSA law has many loopholes, but it does permit Met Council to draw a regional boundary of sorts.

Four years later, after the creation of the Met Council, the state added to its structure of regionalism by adopting the now-well-known tax-sharing law. Despite its widespread reputation as a shining example, the tax-sharing law is actually rather modest. It does not call for jurisdictions to share all property taxes within the region. Rather, it merely requires local jurisdictions to place 40 percent of the growth of their commercial and industrial property-tax base into a regional pool, to be redistributed to jurisdictions on a per capita basis.

At first, this law produced a modest amount of money. Over time, however, the regional pool has grown, and now it redistributes several hundred million dollars a year from tax-rich jurisdictions to tax-poor jurisdictions. Furthermore, the wealth has not been uniformly transferred from the suburbs to the older central cities. In some years, the central city of Minneapolis—with a strong downtown and still-elegant residential neighborhoods—has been a net donor to the pool. And, as with most other metropolitan areas, the Twin Cities region includes dozens of older suburbs that have a modest tax base, which are net financial winners under the tax-sharing law. Overall, the law has reduced the fiscal disparity between the richest and poorest jurisdictions in the region from 50:1 to 12:1.

With a growing regional economy, an independent Metropolitan Council charged with regional planning, and the tax-sharing law in place, the Twin Cities region was viewed—and viewed itself—as a model of regional planning and cooperation. In the early 1990s, however, the question of regional equity was reopened, largely through the efforts of a young state legislator named Myron Orfield, who began to investigate the geographical patterns of public investment within the region. Using the emerging power of computer mapping, Orfield showed that, even under the Met Council system, transportation and other infrastructure investments were being invested disproportionately in fast-growing, high-income, low-density suburbs. Orfield introduced a series of bills calling for sweeping changes in metropolitan governance, fiscal policy, transportation, and land-use planning, with a strong emphasis on affordable housing in all regional communities. Orfield also published a nationally acclaimed book, *Metropolitics,* documenting the need for such policies.

Like his predecessors who had passed the original tax-sharing law, Orfield was called a communist and worse. But his ideas soon caught on with other prominent politicians, among them Ted Mondale, a well-known state senator and son of the former vice president. Encouraged by such political action, the Met Council drew up a new Regional Blueprint in 1994 that specifically calls for giving priority on regional infrastructure investments to communities that have "implemented plans to provide their share of the region's low- and moderate-income and life-cycle housing opportunities." This Blueprint, along with the Urban Service Area requirement, gives the Met Council considerable power over local governments. For example, shortly after the passage of the Blueprint, the Met Council forced Maple Grove, an affluent, low-density suburb, to agree to the construction of higher-density housing, including some rental units, in exchange for the Met Council's approval of a $43 million sewer interceptor.

The Twin Cities' approach to regionalism suggests a steady, though gradual, movement toward consciousness as a Regional City. Recently, however, Minnesota leaders have recognized that, even with fairly strong state-led regionalism, they cannot truly transform their metropolis into a Regional City without a strong commitment to designing the region affirmatively. The tax-sharing law, the Regional Blueprint, and the Metropolitan Urban Service Area all provide the region with mechanisms to improve social and economic equity. But sprawl remains a problem, as does local resistance in affluent suburbs.

Therefore, as the millennium approached, Minnesota took the next step toward creating a true Regional City in the Twin Cities. The state's unconventional governor, Jesse Ventura—former mayor of the older working-class suburb of Brooklyn Park—announced a Smart Growth policy and appointed Ted Mondale to head the Met Council. Together, Ventura and Mondale began focusing on the hard-core physical-design issues associated with metropolitan growth in the Twin Cities—especially the idea of a regional rail system and compact, higher-density development in the region's many centers. In contrast with Salt Lake City, the Twin Cities regional design may be the final step, rather than the first one—building on three decades of regional policy making on growth issues.

All three state-led efforts at regionalism described here teach the same lessons. First, the transformation of our metropolitan areas into Regional Cities is unlikely to occur without strong state leadership on growth issues. Second, regional policies alone cannot do the job, even if they are promoted and supported by strong political leadership at the state level. Only if those policies (and the infrastructure investments that go along with them) are married to a regional and neighborhood design vision can the transformation into a Regional City succeed.

PART FOUR:
RENEWING THE REGION'S COMMUNITIES

The zoning maps that prescribe growth and redevelopment must be refashioned into documents that recognize and reinforce connections between uses. A new language is developing for town and city planning that uses the basic building blocks of community to create a map of places rather than zones.

INTRODUCTION

None of the regional visions, policies, or investments would mean much if they didn't shape our communities at the most basic level: neighborhoods. The transition away from sprawl and urban disinvestment requires rethinking the form and function of the places in which we live. Throughout any region, there are many types of neighborhoods, villages, and towns. Each will have a different dynamic of change. Each will need to develop its own vision of community and the built environment. And each will have to find a way to tap into the emerging Regional City. But all will progress toward greater diversity, more walkable environments, and a more compact, urban form.

This part of the book focuses on three primary conditions: the existing suburb, new growth areas at the edge, and distressed urban neighborhoods and districts. Certainly, many other places will need unique forms of change—such as rural villages or stable urban neighborhoods. The conditions and sites investigated here, however, go to three of the dominant opportunities for change in the region: Suburban Greyfields, Exurban Greenfields, and Urban Brownfields. The urban neighborhood and the regional edge have historically been the focus of many design and policy innovations. The maturing suburb is a relatively new topic and one that is pivotal in the creation of coherent Regional Cities.

The transformation of our existing suburbs, whether first-ring or newer areas, is fundamental to realizing a healthier regional form. In most regions, the existing suburbs now house more than 50 percent of the population. Changing the character of those places by rebuilding their most underutilized areas affords a necessary and rich opportunity. We believe that the most dysfunctional aspects of the postwar suburb can be repaired through infill and selective redevelopment. The housing opportunities can diversify, mobility can be enhanced, and the lack of connections can be mended. The core of the opportunity lies in redeveloping the suburb's strip commercial areas—the "greyfields" of asphalt that can be recycled into village and town cores that serve the adjacent neighborhoods while accommodating new housing.

In addition to the place-by-place remaking of the suburbs, larger institutional change and infrastructure shifts must take place. The zoning maps that prescribe growth and redevelopment must be refashioned into documents that recognize and reinforce connections between uses. A new language is developing for town and city planning that uses the basic building blocks of community to create a map of places rather than zones.

In addition to refashioning the codes, suburban transit will be necessary to weave the region together. The next generation of transit will have to connect suburb to suburb as well as suburbs to central cities. Transit is not only an end in itself, but a framework for organizing redevelopment and infill throughout the region and, perhaps more important, a way of enhancing the pedestrian life of individual neighborhoods and centers.

Regardless of Regional Boundaries and policies to support infill and redevelopment, many regions will continue to have some part of their growth at the exurban fringe. This growth must be integrated into the Regional City, by location, connection, and form. Greenfield development can follow the same urban-design principles so relevant in the city and the maturing suburbs.

Ironically, these edge sites probably will have a harder time achieving the urban qualities that seem to be gaining ground in other areas. They will have to struggle with market forces that push for uniformly low-density housing. They will have a harder time creating mixed-use centers because the need for retail and other commercial uses is weakest in the outlying areas. And they will be hard pressed to justify transit and truly walkable streets without the diversity and density enjoyed naturally by more central neighborhoods. However, in areas with strong regional policies to set limits to sprawl and clearly define the direction of growth, new greenfield projects can intensify in ways that areas without limits cannot support. The health of new growth, like the viability of infill, depends on a clear vision of the region.

The revitalization of depressed inner-city neighborhoods has been a long-standing goal for many administrations and civic groups. Partly through the lens of regionalism and partly through the design principles of groups such as the Congress for New Urbanism, a different approach is emerging. As demonstrated by HUD's Consolidated Planning and HOPE VI programs, this new approach builds on the age-old urban-design philosophy of diversity, human scale, and preservation while bringing into practice the notion that the city cannot be divorced from its surroundings. The economic and physical isolation of many inner-city neighborhoods must give way to a regionwide integration of opportunities in jobs and housing.

These, then, are the opportunities for change in the Regional City. Neighborhood by neighborhood, the brownfields and greyfields will redevelop in existing communities, adding a new layer of urbanism to places too often lacking diversity and human scale. Even at the edge, Greenfield development can reinforce the region's evolution toward a more compact, transit-friendly form. Each of these three opportunities is ultimately where the meaning and value of the Regional City expresses itself in our everyday lives.

CHAPTER 9:

THE SUBURB'S MATURATION

Since their creation, the suburbs have been evolving and changing. From bedroom communities to Edge Cities, the trend has been toward more complex and complete places. In the past two generations, employment and retail have followed housing to the suburbs. Now market forces are diversifying the mix of housing types and calling for alternatives to the car. As we have pointed out, walkable neighborhoods and urban centers are emerging as socially desirable, environmentally sound, and economically profitable. The once-segregated places of the suburbs are beginning to be connected by strategic mixed-use projects on infill and redevelopment sites. A network of centers that are urban in the best sense of the word is beginning to overlay and transform the suburban landscape.

But suburban infill has a unique set of problems and constraints. Typically, no-growth and slow-growth advocates oppose infill projects with any density or mixed use—driving the cost of such development ever upward by delays and litigation. Local politics are often oriented to the status quo, and once an area's character has been established, it is hard to change without a powerful consensus. Furthermore, the existing suburban street systems and zoning codes block the creation of different types of developments even when such a consensus is achieved. Finally, the standard density and configuration of suburbia make transit a heavily subsidized safety net rather than a functional alternate to the car.

If we are to direct significant growth to suburban infill locations, much must change. Foremost, citizens must understand that there are options for growth other than more sprawl—and a clear picture of these alternatives must be communicated. Often the simple act of delineating the scale and character of walkable centers and neighborhoods is enough to relieve local anxiety about development. Local concerns must be tempered with regional needs for an equitable distribution of affordable housing and jobs, for the preservation of open space and agriculture lands, and for transit. This calls for a regional process that can both educate and guide the complex interaction of economics, ecology, tectonics, jurisdiction, and social equity. Without public education and clarity on the real alternatives, suburban infill options may be stranded between regional interests and local fears for some time to come.

Four areas must change for the suburbs to mature into more inclusive, complex places. First, each town needs to rework its comprehensive plan and zoning ordinance to allow mixed-use development and to encourage a wider range of housing.

Restructuring each town plan into places rather than zones is a fundamental implementation step of any regional vision. Second, key infill and redevelopment sites must be identified and supported through infrastructure investment and policy. These infill sites are the keys to changing the character of our existing suburbs. Third, Greenfield sites that are determined to be appropriate areas for metropolitan expansion must be planned to be pedestrian friendly, transit accessible, and balanced. Finally, the suburban areas of the region need to be woven together with a diverse transit system, combining trunk-line rail systems with buses, bikeways, and walkable station areas. Each of these four areas of change is critical to the ongoing maturation of the suburbs.

RESTRUCTURING THE SUBURBAN TOWN PLAN

Towns have the same fundamental building blocks as those of regions, and need to use them to revise their comprehensive plans and zoning ordinances. The building blocks of towns are places and links not zones—neighborhoods, districts, corridors, centers, and open-space systems. The contrast between the standard zoning categories and these place-oriented building blocks is dramatic. Residential zones and subdivisions are transformed into neighborhoods scaled to a walk. Shopping centers and office parks are reconceived as mixed-use districts with walkable streets. Arterials and highways can become boulevards with integrated transit. Each of these transformations is possible only when the town begins to see its elements in relation to whole places rather than isolated uses.

Reconceiving an existing town plan by using this structure of places begins to redirect and reshape the location and type of its infill, redevelopment, and new development. It provides a map for the location of neighborhood centers, major mixed-use areas, employment districts, and new open-space systems. Similarly, it reorganizes new growth areas into coherent places and centers. The updated general plan for Palo Alto, California, is a good example of this approach [Plate 35].

The process of remapping our towns requires extensive community participation. Citizens need to take part in the process of defining the town's structure of neighborhoods, centers, corridors, and open space. This process is necessarily a political one, and it must be conducted in a proactive manner. Community participation should be structured around hands-on workshops in which citizens become problem solvers and community designers rather than "problem staters" and armchair critics.

Like regions and neighborhoods, towns need a vital center, clear boundaries, robust circulation networks, and a powerful civic order. These fundamental principles apply across scales, from region to town to neighborhood. A town without a thriving center lacks the economic and cultural crossroads of its community. A town without boundaries soon becomes a sprawling expanse of subdivisions and malls. Without a sense of public space and civic focus, any town can lose its character and identity. Such boundaries, centers, and human-scaled public spaces are no longer the components of our land-use plans—but they need to be.

The suburban town has a hierarchy of centers similar to that of the region, with the addition of the "neighborhood center" to the region's village, town, and urban centers. The neighborhood center is the most basic and most problematic. A neighborhood that maintains a walkable scale is rarely more than 120 acres (a quarter mile or five-minute walk in any direction). In a suburban town, this area will typically include only three hundred to, at a maximum, eight hundred homes. Because the local grocery store is no longer a small mom-and-pop shop, it is hard to find a retail anchor for a market area so small.

Clearly, each neighborhood center cannot have its own full-service grocery store or the smaller shops that logically cluster around it. Smaller increments of retail must in some cases be subsidized as a community amenity if they are to succeed. The neighborhood center therefore must become a mix of civic uses (such as a day-care center, a senior center, or an elementary school) along with a neighborhood green and whatever stores are feasible. Often, a simple shared open space is enough to create identity for a neighborhood, even if it doesn't put shopping or jobs within walking distance.

The problem is partly due to the fact that the stores have grown so big and partly due to our rushed lifestyles. We need to be able to run many errands in one place because we are so pressed for time. This amounts to a retail center of at least 100,000 square feet, including a major grocery store, a hardware store, and a drugstore. These retail centers become what we call village centers if they are designed as walkable environments with civic and other uses mixed in. A town may have several village centers, depending on its population. Village centers are logical places for multifamily and senior housing. They also provide opportunities for smaller, local-serving office space: doctors, dentists, travel agencies, and the like. Some smaller civic uses, such as a branch library, post office, or youth center, also are appropriate. Village centers are the smallest increment that would show up on a regional plan and have been described as one of the regional building blocks.

Town centers, too, are regional building blocks, but in a town plan they form the heart of the municipality. Whatever is most unique about a town should be expressed here. There are some traditional qualities that most town centers need. They must be twenty-four-hour districts with activities and services for day use and night life. They will typically have the greatest residential densities of the town and be the crossroads for the area's transit system. They should have the greatest concentration of jobs (but, given twenty-five years of building office parks at freeway exit ramps, they often do not). Walkable town centers are what all the homebuyer surveys indicate people now want to live near or in, but sadly such places are the exception and not the rule.

The other building blocks of the region need to be incorporated and reinforced in each town plan. Corridors, both natural and human-made, form the linkages within the town and to the region. They, along with the centers, are a prime opportunity for mixed-use infill within a new town structure—where strip commercial is replaced with walkable centers. Districts also are a part of the town structure. They provide for the special uses that cannot be integrated into neighborhoods or centers.

A Taxonomy of Suburban Towns

There are several types of suburban towns, depending largely on their age and location. The older first-ring suburbs produced towns before World War II that in many cases were connected to the city by streetcars or rail lines. This transit basis gave them an innate pedestrian orientation and scale. They were designed around people walking to the station and stopping at various places along the way. They had all the characteristics of good urban design without the challenges of contemporary lifestyles and economies.

Today, these towns are either very desirable or rundown and neglected. The difference lies in their location. Chris Lienberger, of the respected real estate economic firm Charles Lessor, has identified the "favored quarter" of a region: the quadrant of suburban growth emanating from the historic city that captures most of the new jobs and higher-income households. The favored quarter is easy to identify and map in any region of the country. Within these preferred regional quadrants, historic towns and streetcar suburbs become highly valued community centers. Such town centers are now beginning to attract all the uses that had been sprawling in the Edge City's office parks and retail centers. For example, in the San Francisco Bay area, the upscale shops and start-up businesses would all rather be in downtown Palo Alto or Mountain View than out at the freeway.

In the other regional quarters, historic streetcar towns are not faring so well—they are the first-ring suburbs in decline. Home to blue-collar communities that first fled the city, they are in danger of repeating the city's downward cycle—fewer jobs, lower tax base, poor services, declining schools, and little investment. This decline is particularly threatening because these towns lack much of the intrinsic and historic value of the city. Here, Main Street is largely vacant, the train station is closed, and many historic buildings have been destroyed or are in decay. From an urban design standpoint, these towns had much that is desirable. But, from a regional standpoint, they are out of the economic flow. And without local economic revitalization or the regional policies previously described—tax-base sharing, regional boundaries, new transit investments, targeted employment centers, and better schools—no amount of good urban design will save them.

Moving outward in the region, we come to the suburbs that were built after World War II. These towns literally have no center or history. If you ask a resident to take you to the town center, more often than not you will end up in a mall. These towns are connected to the region and the city only by highways; little or no transit or rail works in such areas. Often, they were planned with large single-use zones knitted together with four- and six-lane arterials. Somewhere along the arterials is a civic center surrounded by parking. These are the towns that can be most easily transformed by redeveloping their greyfields of asphalt into town and village centers.

These centerless towns also take on different characteristics, depending on their location in the region. In the high-growth sections, these towns are riddled with gated communities, golf courses, upscale shopping centers, and massive office parks. These areas are the least likely to change, because of their wealth and desire to remain exclusive. The diversity advocated by a Regional City plan is too radical and inclusionary for most of these towns. Mixed-use centers with multifamily housing are falsely seen as inviting crime and undesirable elements into their communities. The strategy that these towns tend to prefer is to limit growth and build bigger roads.

Beyond the suburban edge are freestanding towns that are quickly being drawn into the economic constellation of the region. Historically, these towns were agricultural in the West and single-industry towns in the East. As those original economies have waned, many of the towns have suffered population declines and economic stagnation. A few, largely with small colleges or universities, have become communities of choice for the ultramobile workers of the information economy. Their mix of higher education and a high quality of life is attracting high-end small businesses and independent workers.

These towns are particularly interested in controlling sprawl and rebuilding their town centers. To maintain their prosperity, they need to offer a different environment from that of the Edge City suburb. They need to preserve the natural features that are so desirable to most people with choice, and they need to create a vital town center that offers high-quality entertainment, shopping, and culture within a walking environment.

Most suburban towns are a mix of prewar core areas and postwar edges—they are a microcosm of the region. Each has a historic core with an old train station (now typically a restaurant), a run-down Main Street, and old grid-street neighborhoods close by. At the bypass highway is a mall or a power center, with some apartments across a big arterial and, just beyond, a series of subdivisions.

If you study the traffic patterns in this hybrid town, more often than not you will find that the worst traffic congestion is in the newer, low-density areas. The old street-grid part of town has parallel routes and distributes the traffic better. In the new parts, the arterials are congested because all trips are forced through them. And, as has been described, the strip is lined with parking lots and commercial ripe for redevelopment.

In the wealthier towns, the historic Main Street has been filled with new shops (but the train station is still a restaurant) and the older neighborhoods have been renovated. In the poorer towns, not much has happened in the center, and many of the older malls and shopping centers are closing. Without a regional plan that values the social capital of these towns, such places will continue in slow decline.

Some towns, especially the old freestanding towns about to be engulfed by the edges of the metropolis, are trying to construct Greenbelts to hold back sprawl. In some cases they vote for Greenlines meant to prevent the town itself from sprawling out into the next town. This strategy needs a cooperative county that will enforce a no-build policy on the lands outside of the line. These local Greenlines, or Community Separators, can be very effective at creating edges and identity for a town. And, if properly placed, they can become an important part of the regional open-space network. Access to the open space at the edge of a town can be one of the major attractions for infill and redevelopment within the town.

But often the towns with the political will to create a Greenline also have the political will to become exclusionary in their zoning. They block the infill that should complement the open space and push the development farther to the edge of the metropolis. Boulder, Colorado, is a good example. Its Greenbelt is beautiful and the town, with its university, is a very desirable place to live. But infill housing and commercial development are too often blocked, leaving the town with a poor jobs-to-housing balance and little affordable housing. This ultimately spreads more development into less-controlled neighboring towns and county lands.

A local Greenbelt without proactive infill policies actually fuels sprawl. Here a regional design can help with policies to create and protect the Greenbelts while supporting infill and redevelopment. A regional framework can tie the two, Greenbelt and infill, together in a way that local politics often cannot.

The typical suburban town is primed for a transformation that rebuilds its best parts and replaces its worst. All this can be best accomplished within the framework of a regional design that coordinates open-space networks, helps to support reinvestment where it is needed, and creates transit options that reinforce the town's creation of walkable places. When this framework has been set, infill and redevelopment of its Greyfields can contribute to both the town's health and the region's compact configuration.

SUBURBAN GREYFIELDS

Suburban Greyfields, the low-density commercial zones known for their relentless surface parking lots and single-story buildings, come in many forms and sizes ripe for redevelopment. Some are large parcels that contained major shopping areas now gone to seed—the dead-mall sites. Many are small individual parcels that line our highways and arterials—the strip commercial zones. And, increasingly there is a special form of suburban Greyfields—surplused military bases and other underutilized institutional areas. Each scale and location presents different challenges and opportunities. All represent one of the prime mechanisms for reshaping the suburban landscape.

Each Greyfield, because of size and location, can take on a different role in the making of a Regional City. Major sites such as a military base or a surplused airport (for example, the old Stapleton Airport in Denver [Plates 24 and 25] can become a series of new neighborhoods or urban centers. Old mall and commercial centers, normally twenty to forty acres, can become new village or town centers with a more complete mix of retail, employment, and housing [Plates 28 and 29]. The smaller strip parcels, however, are more challenging because of their fractured ownership patterns [Plate 30]. In some cases, simply rezoning the smaller parcels for mixed-use buildings at higher densities can spark the redevelopment of a corridor one parcel at a time. In other cases, they need either a redevelopment agency to assemble lots or a cooperative "specific area plan" to develop a comprehensive plan [Plate 38]. One way or another, these corridors can intensify to provide more housing and retail choices for the surrounding residential areas.

In all cases, the goal is a type of infill and redevelopment that creates a greater range of housing and services in the area. Adding jobs, civic facilities, and multifamily and senior housing to an area of single-family homes is a way to balance the neighborhood and create more choice—in housing and in commuting patterns. Adding a pedestrian-friendly focus to an existing auto-oriented environment is another important opportunity. This, in combination with housing, retail, and civic elements, can create a new center for neighborhoods once isolated by strip commercial and inhospitable streets.

The larger Greyfield sites such as military bases or other large institutional sites represent opportunities to create whole neighborhoods and commercial districts [Plates 21–23]. Because of their central location, their market can support a greater variety of housing and retail than can a similar-sized Greenfield site at the edge of town. Because of this locational strength, major infill sites are particularly important assets to a regional plan.

A ubiquitous redevelopment opportunity for most suburban towns is the reuse of old strip commercial areas and dead-mall sites. They have the advantage of being located centrally within each community and are easily accessible to transit. And they have the advantage of not being directly within the residential areas that they serve. They are often eyesores that few would defend and many would like to see transformed. Many of these strip commercial sites lining the suburb's arterials have outlived their economic life and market value but are hostage to single-use low-density zoning. They are available for redevelopment because retail is the fastest changing segment of the development industry.

Every decade seems to bring a new model of how we shop. After World War II, the downtown department stores and old town-center Main Streets were replaced by suburban malls, strip commercial arterials, and grocery-anchored "neighborhood" centers. As our housing shifted to the suburbs, the form of retail that followed it changed dramatically. Since that fundamental shift to the suburbs, the format, grouping, and scale of the shops continued to evolve—most typically into larger formats and more focused groupings. The Urban Land Institute (ULI) developed a taxonomy of suburban retail types that is constantly updated. The list now includes convenience centers, festival market centers, entertainment centers, community centers, neighborhood centers, outlet centers, power centers, discount centers, and, of course, malls.

Additionally, retail is typically overbuilt—but this is merely a manifestation of the rapidly changing types. The old centers are slowly being vacated as new centers gain their clientele. The resulting underutilized shopping areas can fester, leading to lost taxes and contributing to the ultimate decay of the neighborhood or town. This was the pattern for many inner cities, and it can easily become the pattern for many first-ring suburbs—lower retail tax revenues leading to poorer services with higher residential and business taxes.

Three new retail formats are currently displacing the present forms of suburban shopping: big-box power centers, e-tail, and the reemergence of Main Street. These new forms are undermining the older malls and strip centers, as they are changing the nature of our communities and our lives.

Power centers are the hypersuburban form, perhaps the climax stage of suburban retail, to borrow an ecological term. They are 100 percent auto oriented, megascaled, single use, and remote. Their size (often as much as 500,000 to 800,000 square feet for all the stores) means that they draw from a market area as large as seven miles. They are a format that offers value (lower-cost products) and convenience (easy parking). They are cannibalizing local hardware, grocery, stationary, pet, toy, and drug stores. At the same time, they are sucking up the dollars spent in most of the older strip retail centers. They are vilified by some community groups because they are often the death knell for many historic Main Streets and older local stores. But it is important to acknowledge that they serve an important need—especially for lower-income families.

Newer yet is e-tailing, shopping on the Internet. To date, it constitutes just 1 percent of retail activity and is projected by some to climb to just 3 percent by 2005. In a way, e-tailing is much like power-center retailing; both are backed up by huge warehouses stocking large volumes of products at low prices. But, instead of being picked up at a warehouse, the products are delivered to people's homes. If the software works, it can offer the ultimate in convenience and affordability. It is much more energy efficient to move delivery vans than individual cars. And it will save people time.

Two factors will limit e-tail, however. First, people have a natural desire to see and feel the merchandise. Reinforcing this desire is the reality that, for many, shopping is a social experience and, in many cases, has entertainment value. The desire to browse in a real place rather than on-screen is powerful. Second, many, in fact most, of the lower-income households that now shop at the power centers are not on the Internet. If they get there, then start looking for the redevelopment of the power centers in the near future; they will be the next set of Greyfields. If they don't, then power centers and e-tailing will be bookends of the retail world.

The remaining retail will focus on the experience of shopping, a sense of place, and the entertainment aspect of going out. To lure people away from the convenience and values on the computer screen, shopping areas will have to relearn the lessons of historic Main Streets: beauty, human scale, diversity, sociability, and fun. And they will have to be mixed use, adding civic uses, housing, and offices.

In fact, the rebirth of Main Street shopping is well underway even without the fallout from e-tailing or power centers. It is the third major trend in retail currently affecting our communities. The rejuvenation of historic Main Streets and town centers is ubiquitous wherever average household incomes are high. In these upscale markets, new or redeveloped Main Streets are a natural evolution.

But, in lower-income areas, Main Streets are struggling—vacancies are typically high and maintenance is low. Given that many of the finest historic Main Streets are located in lower-income areas, support should be developed for their preservation and revitalization. In these struggling areas, Business Improvement Districts (BIDs) can be employed to manage and maintain the street as if it were a shopping center. Under such cooperative management, the tenant mix can be designed to reinforce the whole experience, and empty shops, which can easily create a negative environment for nearby stores, are quickly filled. The historic architecture and natural human scale in older Main Streets are features that most people are drawn to if the street is safe, clean, and free of vacancies. The added security and maintenance paid for by the BID are critical to making the street feel safe and cared for.

Along with historic Main Street restorations, new Main Streets are emerging, but in hybrid configurations. Lacking the central location of historic Main Streets, the new Main Streets need major activity generators, such as a cinema complex, a cluster of "lifestyle" shops, or a large grocery store. The mixing of an auto-oriented anchor and a pedestrian-oriented Main Street is quickly becoming a new retail type. [Plate 38, Mountain Avenue Revitalization Plan, as an example of mixing cinema with a new Main Street.] In some cases, these hybrid Main Streets can be located in older commercial areas that are redeveloping. In other cases, they can form the town center of a new development. [Plate 37, Issaqua Highlands, as an example of a new Main Street town center.] In all cases, these new Main Streets need to be mixed use—office, civic, and residential developments need to be integrated and close at hand.

The Greyfields of suburbia will move in many directions. Some will evolve into mixed-use villages and town centers, others will become more intensive employment or residential areas, and still others will redevelop in more standard retail configurations at higher densities. But the fact remains that the Greyfields produced by low-density strip development and older retail formats are an abundant opportunity to reform the suburbs.

There are other opportunities for infill and redevelopment in the suburban environment—other types of Greyfields. Underutilized institutional lands located in key areas are major opportunities in some communities. Certainly, there are some purely residential districts in need of infill and redevelopment. Office parks also can be transformed by mixed-use infill development as their surface parking lots are shared or structured. Just as the city has its Brownfields of older industrial districts as a prototypical redevelopment opportunity, the suburb has its Greyfields. Transforming the character of the typical arterial with its apron of parking lots is not only an opportunity; it is the signature of the maturation of the suburbs.

EXURBAN GREENFIELDS

The controversy over the quantity and location of new growth is often at the heart of regional design. As has been described earlier in this book, the regional-design process must arrive at a complex trade-off between a hypothetical free-market ideal and other public concerns. In an ideal world, Greenfield development would logically follow transit and infrastructure opportunities while avoiding critical open-space networks. And it would be limited. But we do not live in an ideal world.

In many regions, infill and redevelopment cannot handle all the pressures for growth. Even with a healthy percentage of investment moving toward existing communities, new Greenfield areas for development need to be sensitively located and planned. An important "layer" of a regional design is the placement and size of such Greenfield development sites. The quantity of these sites must be delicately balanced between demonstrated growth demands and the need to make infill development a priority.

Some advocates of sprawl claim that few if any constraints should apply to Greenfield development—that the marketplace will effectively allocate the correct placement and size of new development. However, the free-market allocation of Greenfield sites is not without bias. Two forces often overextend development and distort the market-place's allocation.

First and foremost, land speculation on farmlands and open space is very profitable and therefore tends to distort the allocation of development. In California's Sacramento County, for example, the price of farmland is often just $5,000 to $10,000 an acre, whereas the value of land zoned for development can be well over $80,000 an acre. A windfall profit margin. Speculators make a lot of money betting on which lands will be converted into urban uses without necessarily providing a comparable investment in infrastructure or public services. In some cases, they spend a lot of money on local elections.

Such speculation certainly distorts the location and size of development at the edges of the region. While speculators extract values created largely by the public's ability to rezone land, homebuilders and ultimately the homebuyers are left to cover the hard expenses of such development. Either the public should share in the incremental value created by the rezoning or the farmlands should be preserved.

The second force that pushes development to Greenfields in a distorted manner is the difficulty and expense of infill development. Building within existing communities and having to respond to fearful neighbors without a supportive regional consensus are often major barriers for developers. Because many citizens incorrectly believe that the answer to sprawl is to limit growth near them, the process of infill development is arduous, time consuming, risky, and expensive. For many builders, it is cheaper, more certain, and faster to buy land at the edge and pay for speculative land prices, new infrastructure, and services.

It is the supreme irony of our current political system that we subsidize Greenfield development by giving away the value created by rezoning open space or farmlands while we create disincentives to infill with a public approval process that is arduous and risky.

Regional design can help to reverse this pattern. The public "gift" of rezoning Greenfields and providing infrastructure should be compensated by significant contributions to public services and infrastructure costs. The cost and risk of infill should be reduced by zoning that supports redevelopment in appropriate areas. This reversal—increasing the difficulty of Greenfield development and easing the infill—can be one of the most significant results of the regional-design process. It can remove the open-market speculation on Greenfields and create a positive environment for infill.

Where Greenfield development is appropriate, its design should follow the same principles that we have articulated for infill development—walkable neighborhoods that are diverse in everyday uses and housing opportunities. Ironically, achieving this diversity in use and housing is often more challenging in more remote areas. Greenfield sites, because there is little around them, have a hard time creating a critical market for retail. They also have a difficult time capturing a market for townhomes and apartments, because the desirability of such housing is nurtured by proximity to job centers, services, and mature urban environments. In too many cases, Greenfield developments end up with a void in which the town-center retail, jobs, and multifamily housing wait for market demand to catch up.

Greenfield new towns are more likely to succeed as complete places when their numbers are limited. A good example is Issaquah Highlands [Plates 36 and 37], located seventeen miles east of Seattle. Because Puget Sound's regional plan limits such sites, the market will support a full range of housing and commercial types. In fact, 60 percent of the housing is multifamily, and one-third of all the housing will be affordable. Its commercial development is strengthened by public investments (a major new north-south arterial) and by the fact that Microsoft is planning its second major campus for approximately 15,000 employees in its town center.

In fact, the developer of Issaquah Highlands, Port Blakely Communities, believes that the market for the planned community's more compact form, mixed uses, walkability, and higher densities is a healthy result of the state's growth-management law. Without regional growth management, it would undoubtedly be a very different place. If competing commercial development were allowed to sprawl, the townlike form of

Issaquah Highlands would not be possible. If housing were unconstrained in the area, this site might have become a large-lot subdivision complete with golf course and gates. Instead, a diverse, compact new town is under construction.

A particularly instructive aspect of the project is the way in which it deals with a major arterial passing through its town center. The problem of such roads subdividing a town or bypassing them is endemic in much of the suburbs. Major retail centers need arterials (often four to six lanes) for access and visibility, but such roads are barriers to the pedestrian and breed standard strip retail configurations. At Issaquah, the intersecting arterials are split into four one-way streets to form an urban grid. In this way, they maintain a pedestrian-friendly character at the same time that they carry similar volumes of traffic. Because of the smaller scale of the one-way streets, the buildings of the town can front directly on the sidewalks and reinforce the urban identity of the place. Additionally, this configuration allows more of the major stores visibility from the high-volume streets. It is an urban street strategy brought to the suburbs to help in town making.

A surprising result of this road system is that it moves traffic more efficiently than does the standard arterial intersection. In detailed traffic modeling, the couplet resulted in a shorter overall travel time through the town center, because all the left turns are "free"—they turn from a one-way street onto another. As we have all experienced, the waiting time at a standard intersection is long because of the time needed to clear the left-turn pockets. The left-turn pockets also widen the intersection at the expense of the pedestrian. The couplet has no need of them; it offers a better pedestrian environment, better traffic flow, and better retail visibility.

At 30,000 acres, the Southeast Orlando Plan [Plate 34] is a larger example of planning for a greenfield site. This area surrounding the Orlando International Airport is a logical and perhaps an inevitable development area for the Orlando region. The airport and its dependent industrial area form a major employment center, and the existing infrastructure provides an efficient framework for new growth. As they should be, the jobs and infrastructure were primary factors in selecting the area for new development.

The process used in developing the plan is as instructive as the results. First, the site's extensive wetlands and habitat were mapped and designated as preserves. Greenbelts were added to these preserved lands to connect them into a continuous open-space network, drainage system, and habitat-protection area. This open-space network then formed the primary framework for the rest of the development. The circulation system, including rail transit, was layered onto this framework. Finally, these two networks, natural and circulation, formed the foundation for a series of districts, neighborhoods centers, village centers, and town centers. The design proceeded from environmental opportunities to infrastructure planning to the urban design of the centers.

The urban design of each center was controlled by a flexible new planning technique called *block standards*. These standards gave the developers flexibility in design and mix of uses while ensuring that each center would develop into a walkable, mixed-use place. The standards identified four block types that could make up any center: residential blocks, civic blocks, commercial blocks, and, most important, mixed-use blocks. They gave a range of uses and densities for each block type. The mixed-use blocks were intended to incorporate most of the significant retail in each center along with housing and office. Commercial blocks were intended primarily to accommodate office and other employment uses but allowed some ground-floor retail. Residential blocks also allowed some other uses but focused primarily on a range of residential densities. The civic blocks provided for parks, public uses, and civic institutions.

The standards gave a range for the proportion of each type of block in each type of center. A neighborhood center would have proportionately more residential blocks, whereas a town center would have more commercial and mixed-use blocks. A village center would have enough mixed-use blocks to provide for a grocery-anchored retail area. Each type of center was given an approximate size in relation to its expected uses and intensities. Varying the density of the blocks and the proportion of the four basic block types enabled virtually any type of urban environment to be created.

In addition, each type of block was assigned other simple standards: a maximum block size, building height limits, maximum parking limits, and, most critical, a minimum amount of "build to lines"—that is, the proportion of the block that must have a building at the sidewalk. Each of these standards was meant to reinforce the urban quality of the centers. Blocks cannot grow to a size uncomfortable for a pedestrian; building heights are in proportion to the scale of the center; parking cannot overwhelm the site; and the buildings have to shape the urban space of the street with active edges. The following table describes the block standards adopted for the Southeast Orlando Plan.

EAST ORLANDO BLOCK STANDARDS

	Town Center	Village Center	Neighborhood Center
Mixed-Use Blocks	20%–80% of Center	25%–70% of Center	12%–25% of Center
Mix of Uses*	Retail, Services, Restaurants, Office, Cinema, Grocery, Hotel, Residential, Civic, Park/Plaza	Grocery, Local-Serving Retail, Restaurants, Professional Offices, Residential, Civic, Park/Plaza	Small Retail/Market[†], Restaurant/Cafe, Civic, Residential, Park/Plaza
Maximum Block Size	7 acres	7 acres	3 acres
Minimum FAR	FAR: 0.5	FAR: 0.4	FAR: 0.4
Minimum Frontage	65% of each street	65% of each street	65% of each street
Parking Ratio	3 spaces : 1000 sf.	3 spaces : 1000 sf.	3 spaces : 1000 sf.
Building Height	2 to 10 story	1 to 3 story	1 to 2 story
Commercial Blocks	0%–55% of Center	0%–40% of Center	0%–12% of Center
Allowable Uses	Office, Retail (10% Max)	Office, Retail (10% Max.)	Office
Maximum Block Size	7 acres	3 acres	3 acres
Minimum FAR	FAR: 0.5	FAR: 0.4	FAR: 0.4
Minimum Frontage	65% of each street	65% of each street	65% of each street
Parking Ratio	3 spaces : 1000 sf.	3 spaces : 1000 sf.	3 spaces : 1000 sf.
Building Height	2 to 10 story	1 to 3 story	1 to 2 story
Residential Blocks	15%–70% of Center	25%–65% of Center	52%–78% of Center
Allowable Uses	Apartments, Condos, Townhouses, Bungalows	Apartments, Condos, Townhouses, Bungalows, Small-Lot Single-Family	Apartments, Condos, Townhouses, Bungalows, Small-Lot Single-Family
Maximum Block Size	3 acres	3 acres	3 acres
Density Range	7 to 50 du/ac	7 to 30 du/ac	7 to 25 du/ac
Minimum Frontage	65% of each street	60% of each street	60% of each street
Parking Ratio	1.5 spaces/unit	1.5 spaces/unit	1.5 spaces/unit
Building Height	2 to 5 story	1 to 3 story	1 to 2 story
Civic Blocks	10% of Center	10% of Center	10% of Center
Allowable Uses	Parks, Recreation, Civic, Day Care	Parks, Recreation, Civic, Day Care	Parks, Recreation, Civic, Day Care
Maximum Block Size	3 acres	3 acres	3 acres

*30%–80% retail, cinema, or hotel required each block, 20%–70% other. [†]Max 10,000 sf/block

These block standards mimic the essence of most American cities: a system of complete blocks, a tradition of sidewalk-oriented buildings, and flexibility in use and density. In the eyes of most developers, this flexibility of use and density is a great trade-off for the required "urbanism" of the standards. The beauty of this approach is its simplicity and flexibility.

Greenfield development presents many complex and interesting challenges for the Regional City. Where it is located, how much should be built, what mix of uses should be included, and which urban form should be used are all critical questions. Some can be answered through the regional-design process. Others must be addressed on a local level. In all cases, Greenfield development can and should be configured into walkable neighborhoods, villages, and towns. It should respect and reinforce the regional open-space system and transit opportunities. It should seek to provide a reasonable balance of jobs to housing, along with a fair proportion of affordable housing. If these simple (if politically challenging) prescriptions are met, Greenfield development can be transformed from sprawl into a healthy component of the Regional City.

SUBURBAN TRANSIT: NOT AN OXYMORON

Since the demolition of America's streetcars in the 1940s and 1950s, transit, particularly in the suburbs, has been more a safety net than a true alternative to the car. The common belief is that the density and urban form of most of our communities cannot support transit in any convenient form or frequency. Rail transit is believed to be too expensive and ill suited to the contemporary metropolis. Our suburban destinations are too dispersed and our primary bus transit systems, running on congested arterials and highways, are too slow to be an attractive alternative to the auto. As a result, overall transit ridership across the country today is no higher than it was in the 1960s. However, in places that combine land-use policy with transit expansion, such as Portland, transit ridership has increased. Transit is essential to healthy regional growth and neighborhood revitalization. It can and should create the armature for the next generation of more compact and walkable development at the regional scale.

Most traffic engineers now agree that we cannot build enough new road capacity to significantly reduce congestion in many of our major metropolitan areas. Many areas lack the budgets or the available rights-of-way to add significant road capacities. Even if we could afford massive road building and widening, the land-use patterns that such roads propagate quickly generate more traffic. As Maryland governor Parris Glendening has said, "We cannot fool ourselves—or the public—any longer: we can no longer build our way out of our highway congestion problems. It is not an environmentally or financially feasible solution."

In many areas, citizen groups have emerged to oppose highway expansion. Their gut sense is that more capacity will only breed more development and traffic, undermining air quality, access to open space, and the economic vitality of their communities. Not believing a significant shift in travel behavior is possible, many now advocate limiting growth rather than expanding capacity. But such growth limits often drive development farther to the regional edge, leaving behind exclusive suburban pockets of affluence or declining neighborhoods starved for investment and redevelopment—more economic segregation and more sprawl.

Changing land-use patterns alone cannot solve this problem. Walkable neighborhoods without transit, though an improvement over auto-only subdivisions, are incomplete. Convenient suburban transit linking the multicentered regional fabric evolving today is essential to a healthier pattern of growth and redevelopment. But our contemporary transit systems have problems—the costs of new light-rail systems are often too high for the demand in many corridors, commuter trains are too limited in service times and too disruptive to neighborhoods, and the operational expense of expanded bus systems is great. This is the Gordian knot of our next generation of growth: how to coevolve community form and transit in an affordable and convenient relationship. How can we make transportation investments that are cost effective, that support walkable neighborhoods, and that focus economic energy on the revitalization of existing communities?

Transit Choices for the Regional City

Unlike road systems, transit should be conceived in a hierarchical form; starting with walkable and "bikeable" streets supporting local bus routes feeding into trunk transit lines with dedicated rights-of-way. This hierarchy is essential to transit's success. Leave out any element and the system becomes inefficient and inconvenient, resulting in what we now have—systems that need more subsidies than possible and systems that cannot attract a growing ridership. Each element—walkable places, local buses, and convenient trunk lines—is critical. Without walkable and bikeable destinations and origins, transit riders are stranded at each end of their trip. Without local and feeder bus routes, people beyond the walking distance of a station are forced to "park and ride" or just use their cars. Without trunk lines with dedicated rights-of-way and frequent service, the travel time for a transit trip extends to a noncompetitive level.

In the suburbs, walkable neighborhoods are feasible and, as we have demonstrated, are expanding. Local bus service is increasingly effective in the context of these walkable neighborhoods, and feeder bus routes gain efficiency when connected to trunk lines that offer convenient service. Although each system depends on the others, walkable environments are the foundation, and convenient trunk lines are the catalysts. It is important to build every link in the transit chain, yet light rail or its equivalent and walkable destinations are often the critical missing elements in this hierarchy of service.

There are those who would falsely pit bus investments against rail. They claim that when rail-based transit is built, investment in buses is limited and the bus riders themselves are deflected to the rails; thus no net gains in transit ridership are achieved. This argument is plain wrong. In Portland, bus ridership increased with the expansion of the new light-rail systems. More trains enhance bus ridership because the whole system becomes more convenient for the transit rider.

Core routes should have dedicated rights-of-way, either by rail or busways, that allow the transit rider to move more quickly than cars stuck in traffic. Routes with lower ridership that cannot justify the expense of private lanes or tracks will move more slowly but can reach more destinations. Combining feeder buses, express buses, and trunk-line rail is critical to providing a convenient alternative to the car. In some unfortunate cases, the bus and rail systems are managed by independent agencies. Here, the lack of coordination and timing can lead to a system in which each element competes with, instead of enhances, the other. But this is not a justification for the "either/or" mentality of some transit advocates. It merely highlights the imperative to integrate the transit network.

Futuristic systems such as monorails and personalized rapid-transit systems are often held up as the next generation of transit. But we believe the future may lie in simply reinventing the streetcar or light-rail trains of the past and shaping them to the modern suburb. Urban form has always configured itself around transportation systems and innovations. From foot and horse through rail to car, our cities have scaled themselves as much to technology as to culture. If we are rediscovering some of the timeless qualities of our older urban forms and updating them to contemporary situations, perhaps the same will be true of our transit systems. The next revolution in transit may not be high-tech; it may be old-fashioned rail updated to be environmentally clean and scaled to the modern metropolis.

Recently a "new/old" rail technology was developed in Europe under government pressure to reduce transit costs in less-dense areas and rural towns. It effectively combines light-rail cars with on-board engines, eliminating the major construction cost of overhead electrification on new routes. When placed on existing but underutilized track, these light-rail cars can reduce the capital cost of a new transit system dramatically. State-of-the-art technology for the engines allows them to run quietly and pollution free with natural gas or diesel fuel. The lightness of the cars allows them to accelerate and stop more like light rail than heavy commuter trains, and their turning radius allows them to operate in urban environments. Additionally, this new light-rail car is a fuel-efficient and comparatively low-maintenance vehicle. It is a form of transit affordable to the maturing suburbs and perfectly suited to linking suburb to suburb as well as suburb to city.

In addition to its affordability, the most significant aspect of this technology is that the cars can be used on existing tracks. With the consolidation of our old train and freight network, much of our historic track is underutilized or abandoned. These lines are particularly important regional assets because they link the centers of historic small towns and they radiate from the city center. These lines were often the formative network of our regions and now connect the areas that provide the greatest opportunities for redevelopment and infill: our old town centers and underutilized industrial areas. By combining this new technology with these old rights-of-way, we create an opportunity to recycle and reuse industrial Brownfields and older town centers. This combination of technology and track is affordable; it works at the densities appropriate to the maturing suburb; it can be more convenient than driving because of its right-of-way; and it focuses investment into areas that need it the most.

There are two key barriers for such systems and for light rail in general: costly federal standards and inappropriate land use. The allowable systems are too expensive because they are burdened with outmoded federal requirements, and land use in many cases is not integrated effectively. Each constraint reinforces the others to produce systems that are complex, expensive, and slow to realize. Light-rail projects in America are on average twice as expensive as similar systems abroad.

A primary problem is that the Federal Railroad Administration (FRA) applies standards developed for heavy-rail systems to light-rail technology. The so-called 2G standard for buff load requires that a vehicle withstand crash impact energy equal to twice the car's weight. The result is that cars are heavier than they need be. This results in a range of negative consequences: higher capital costs, higher energy use, and higher rates of wear and tear. According to a study by consulting engineer Joe Lewalski, American light-rail vehicles are almost four times as heavy as their European counterparts, with a similar difference in life-cycle costs. And the modifications required by the FRA to meet these standards means that the technology developed elsewhere cannot be used "off the shelf"—a dramatic loss in production efficiency and cost savings.

Even with this higher crash worthiness, light-rail vehicles are not allowed to share tracks with freight trains and other heavy-rail vehicles. Sophisticated control and switching systems that allow joint use of track have been operating in Europe for decades. But, because such an approach is not allowed in the United States, new systems often have to bear the burden of developing their own exclusive rights-of-way rather than sharing existing underutilized track.

The cost and disruption of acquiring and permitting new rights-of-way are part of what makes new transit systems prohibitively expensive. Whereas old tracks often have many existing grade-separated intersections, the cost of building new ones drives the cost for a new light-rail system to $50 million per mile or more. In addition, old tracks are typically less disruptive to existing neighborhoods because they evolved with large setbacks and are typically surrounded by industrial and commercial areas— prime opportunities for redevelopment and infill. In short, existing tracks are perfectly located to prevent the disruption of neighborhoods, to provide safe intersections, to connect historic town centers, and to become catalysts for Brownfield redevelopment.

Suburban transit systems that only chase existing development in hopes of finding riders always come up short. The density and walkability is not there. Instead, new systems should connect prime infill and redevelopment areas within existing town centers to allow more transit-oriented development to evolve. In fact, the land-use pattern in a corridor should be designed to coevolve with the system, both to attract higher ridership and to direct the growth that the added transportation capacity will inspire. Many suburban corridors can achieve a ridership that will make the system operationally efficient only through Transit Oriented Development.

Indeed, every increase in circulation capacity will generate new growth potential, but the type and placement of the growth varies with the technology. We understand how new highway capacity generates new sprawl, but not how some forms of transit can help generate walkable neighborhoods and centers. Ironically, heavy-rail commuter trains and high-speed transit with large park-and-ride facilities often provide an opportunity for more sprawl. Stations accessed primarily by cars, when placed in out-lying areas, can generate sprawl in much the same manner that a new beltway does. For this reason, land use and the transit system must be integrated—and the selection of transit technology and operations is critical to the land-use implications. Transit Oriented Development rather than stations surrounded with parking lots can increase ridership and control the growth effects of new transit systems.

Sonoma–Marin Corridor Study

A perfect example of this approach is provided by a land-use–transportation corridor study for Sonoma and Marin Counties just north of San Francisco. Historically, this area developed first along a single rail line and later along a single highway. The eight towns in the corridor each have historic rail stations at their centers, having grown primarily around the train service that served the area before the construction of the Golden Gate Bridge. The 54-mile corridor has low-density sprawl in most of its new areas, but there is a core of traditional urbanism at the center of each town. It is an interesting footnote that Marin's historic neighborhoods, walkable areas such as Mill Valley and Sausalito, command the greatest real estate values. The older Transit Oriented Developments are now popular in the marketplace.

Because of the area's history, the Sonoma–Marin area's urban form resembles a string of pearls, rather than the sprawl that typically develops around suburban beltways. Its one freeway, however, is very congested and will remain so. The linear regional form that works well for transit doesn't favor the freeway, because auto trips are not dispersed in many directions. In addition to the fact that all the subregion's trips are concentrated onto the single highway, there are few routes parallel to the freeway. This means that short local trips often combine with longer through trips to chronically congest the freeway.

The study looked at five alternative land-use–transportation strategies. The Base Case provided for some highway improvements and modest investments in bus service but for no use of the underutilized tracks and no land-use changes. The second alternative was road oriented and added a new HOV (high-occupancy vehicle) lane for the length of the freeway with increased bus service. It was the most expensive alternative at $834 million. The other three alternatives combined rail service with bus, some HOV, and varying land-use scenarios—each an integrated proposal that combined many transportation strategies.

The first of these integrated proposals included a minimal rail service with commuter-style timing of the trains, some HOV construction, and no land-use changes. This option was the least expensive at $276 million but captured only 5,800 train riders. Adding TODs to this minimal service of trains (every half hour during mornings and evenings) surprisingly doubled the ridership to 11,250 and cost little more at $296 million. The changes in land-use policy to locate more development near the stations was quite modest, representing only a 5 percent shift in housing allocation in Marin and 6 percent in Sonoma. This option showed that supporting transit with development did not require a massive change in land-use policy—but it did greatly enhance the effectiveness of the system. The final option studied the possibility of increasing the rail service to fifteen-minute headways at peak and thirty-minute headways in middays, at night, and on weekends. The ridership doubled again to 24,250, and the capital cost moved to $430 million, still close to half of the highway-only option.

This level of ridership is comparable to that of many new light-rail systems in major cities such as Portland or Sacramento. The surprising difference, given the ridership numbers, is that the Sonoma–Marin system is a suburb-to-suburb system without a downtown destination to anchor it. Such a high ridership demonstrates that the old assumptions about transit—that it needs a major city destination and that its corridor must be high in density—can be revisited. Suburban environments can support rail transit if aided by TODs, if the technology employed is affordable, and if the alternates are congested.

Regardless of the alternative, the freeway remained congested—even in the option that widened the freeway for its entire length. None of the options studied could free the freeway from congestion because of its tendency to attract local as well as long trips. Regardless of the amount of highway expansion or transit alternatives, the highway's capacity was always filled with a combination of trips generated by new development or an endless reserve of local trips eager to use any excess capacity created on the freeway.

This is a hard and critical lesson: transit does not necessarily fix highway congestion. But nothing else can either, for the simple reason that if freeway capacity is available, people will use it. Even with massive road building in quantities well beyond the budgets of most regions, congestion will recede only temporarily. Transit is necessary to give people an alternative to congested highways, not as a means to eliminate auto congestion. The fundamental goal of our transportation policy must shift from free-moving cars to access and mobility.

The technology proposed for the Sonoma–Marin system was a type of light, self-propelled car recently developed in Europe and described earlier. Critical to the Sonoma–Marin corridor, such light-rail cars can move through neighborhoods easily and quietly, they can fit into town streets, and are safe because they can stop like a bus, not like a locomotive. And, unlike the light-rail vehicles typically built in the United States, they are affordable. Whereas the new Portland Westside LRT is projected to cost about $50 million to $60 million per mile, the Sonoma–Marin system would cost about $5 million to $10 million per mile—affordable technology using existing tracks.

Unfortunately, the FRA regulations preclude this technology without substantial modifications—modifications that drive up the cost of production and the cost of operation and maintenance. Nonetheless, the proposed system, similar to a system recently proposed for Pittsburgh, provided very affordable operations, especially when compared with express bus. The study showed that express-bus operation and maintenance would be about $6.80 per trip, whereas rail would be about $2.90. This difference is primarily because the rail allows a higher driver-to-passenger ratio (driver costs are typically as much as 70 percent of operation costs for a transit system). Additionally, trains use less energy and require less maintenance. And the HOV lane construction necessary to make the bus a reasonable alternative to the automobile costs approximately $700 million more than the rail system.

Walk, bike, bus, and rail options were all critical to the Sonoma–Marin system, as was an integrated system. Too often the elements of a complete system are operated by separate agencies that not only fail to coordinate the timing of service, but also compete for funding. Such fractured systems are just another manifestation of the lack of regional coordination and its resulting inefficiencies. Like land use, transit must be designed as an integrated system at a regional scale without artificial jurisdictions.

Much was learned from the options in the study, and this information was used to fashion the final proposal. The preferred system combined investments in each layer of the transportation system. New bikeways, expanded feeder bus service, the new train system, and critical HOV links were included in a ballot initiative for a new sales tax. In addition, money for open-space acquisition and a program for zoning changes was included. However, California had just passed a conservative initiative to limit new taxes by requiring a two-thirds supermajority for any local tax increases. This proved to be too great a hurdle in Sonoma and Marin, as it has in every other similar attempt. Integrated land-use–transportation plans such as this one are still rare and need a supportive state and regional political infrastructure to succeed.

The lessons are clear, however. Land-use policy can have a large effect on transit ridership and the cost effectiveness of transit investments. Suburb-to-suburb patterns of travel can support rail transit. And most auto congestion cannot be solved with more roads or with more transit. What is needed is an integrated solution that provides access and mobility. The goal is to provide more choices in modes of transportation and in types of communities, not more asphalt.

GREYFIELDS/GREENFIELDS

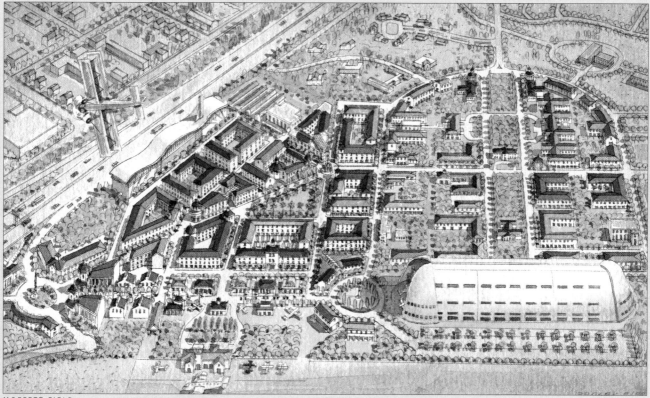

MOFFETT FIELD

[PLATE 21]

Central to constraining sprawl and building coherent regions is the reuse and redevelopment of Suburban Greyfields—underutilized institutional and strip commercial areas. The following projects range from major sites such as decommissioned airports, dead malls, and underutilized military bases to the small-scale redevelopment of individual parcels along decaying arterials. Common to all is an effort to diversify the housing opportunities, mix land uses, and create more pedestrian-friendly environments. Along with such infill sites, each region will need a reasonable proportion of Greenfield development, in appropriate areas, to extend similar urban design traditions.

Moffett Field (shown above) was a major Defense Department facility and airport spread across approximately 1,000 acres along the San Francisco Bay in the heart of what is now Silicon Valley. It is shared by several federal agencies including NASA. The master plan calls for the reuse of a portion of the site near a new light-rail station that connects to downtown San Jose.

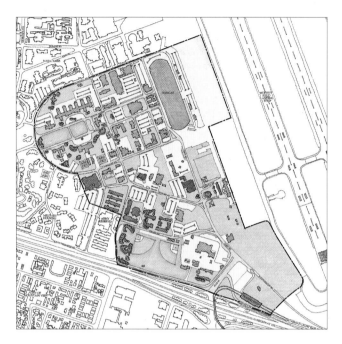

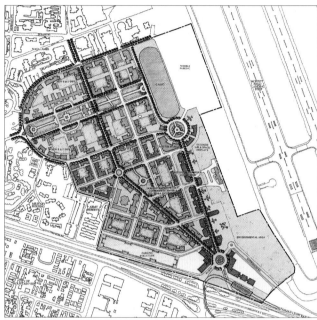

[PLATE 22]
MOFFETT FIELD

MOUNTAIN VIEW,
CALIFORNIA

The redevelopment plan calls for a mix of housing and retail along with the addition of a major university partner for NASA. In addition, the historic WWI blimp hanger will be turned into an Air and Space Museum to function as a regional civic attraction. This is an example of integrating three scales: a national research center, a regional civic facility, and a local mixed-use community.

OPEN SPACE   CIVIC SPACE   EMPLOYMENT   SINGLE-FAMILY   MULTI-FAMILY   COMMERCIAL   = 200 FEET

[PLATE 23]
BAY MEADOWS

SAN MATEO, CALIFORNIA
The reuse of the old racetrack's
surplus land provides a 30-acre
site for the consolidation of
Franklin Fund's headquarters
and 40 acres of mixed-use
development. Franklin Fund's
million-square-foot facility is
developed at considerably
higher density than a typical
suburban campus, but it has the
advantage of being in a mixed-
use area served by transit. The
area is completed with 750 units
of housing, parks, hotel, cinema,
and retail. This is a powerful
example of the changing attitudes
of many major corporations to
favor locating in mixed-use
urban centers.

☐ = 200 FEET

[PLATE 24] STAPLETON AIRPORT REUSE

DENVER, COLORADO

Stapleton is the 4,700-acre airport for Denver that was closed when the larger and more remote Denver International Airport opened in 1995. Following eight years of progressive planning by the Stapleton Development Commission, a major national developer, Forest City, acquired the site. One key to the plan is the structure of its 1,100-acre open space system. The 'day-lighting' of buried creeks and waterways, and their use for water treatment, storm detention, ecological restoration, and human recreation is a powerful complement to the new Stapleton's walkable neighborhoods and major employment centers. The larger open space system includes a series of town greens, neighborhood parks, and pocket parks. The site will ultimately provide 12,000 units of housing and up to ten million square feet of commercial space. At this scale such infill and reuse has a major impact on the direction and extent of regional growth patterns.

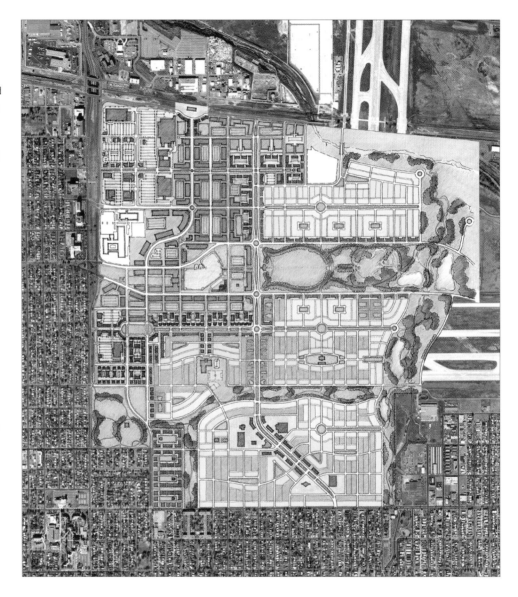

OPEN SPACE   CIVIC SPACE   EMPLOYMENT   SINGLE-FAMILY   MULTI-FAMILY   COMMERCIAL   = 200 FEET

[PLATE 25] **STAPLETON AIRPORT REUSE**

DENVER, COLORADO

Following the traditions of the historic neighborhoods and commercial districts of Denver, the master plan shows multiple new mixed-use neighborhoods, several town centers, and a range of commercial districts. Central to both its residential and commercial districts is an urban design philosophy that creates a comfortable walking environment with a complex mix of uses.

[PLATE 26]
NORTHAMPTON STATE HOSPITAL

NORTHHAMPTON, MASSACHUSETTS

The reuse of the old mental hospital site in Northampton is another example of the history of an area defining the scale and character of infill development. The hospital, founded in 1850, became obsolete but retains significance as a regional landmark. The site is to be redeveloped with a mix of housing, retail, and office uses. True to the traditional community that surrounds it, a connective pedestrian environment and a mixed-use center are the genesis of the new plan. Parts of the historic buildings will be used for a new mental health education center and a hotel with conference and banquet facilities. A traditional Main Street connects these elements and the surrounding town.

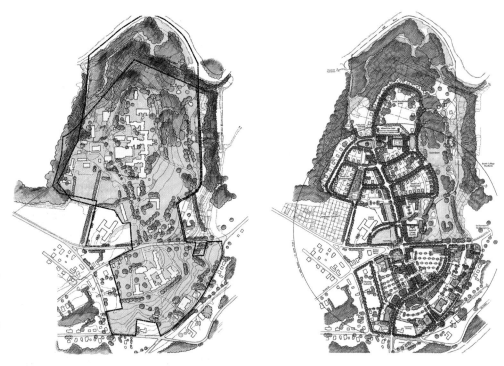

| OPEN SPACE | CIVIC SPACE | EMPLOYMENT | SINGLE-FAMILY | MULTI-FAMILY | COMMERCIAL | ☐ = 200 FEET |

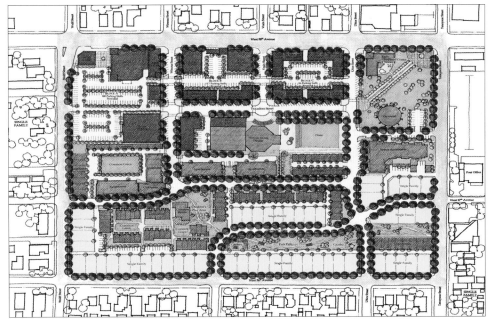

[PLATE 27]

**HIGHLAND'S
GARDEN VILLAGE**

DENVER, COLORADO

The reuse of an old amusement park, Elitch Gardens, is an example of Greyfield redevelopment that reflects the pattern of its surrounding neighborhood while preserving critical historic buildings. An old theater and carousel, through adaptive reuse, will become the focus of the new development. The site will ultimately contain a full range of housing opportunities: single-family, townhomes, live/work lofts, apartments, senior housing, and even a "co-housing" area. Retail, office, community buildings, and a small private school will complete the mix.

☐ = 200 FEET

ROW HOUSES

TOWN HOUSES

APARTMENTS

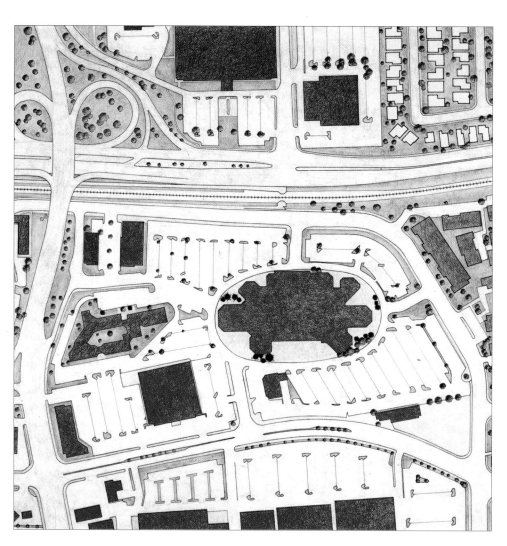

[PLATE 28] THE CROSSINGS

MOUNTAIN VIEW, CALIFORNIA

One of the most plentiful infill opportunities in the suburbs is the redevelopment of dead or underutilized malls. This surplus is partly the product of overbuilding and partly the product of changing retail economies. In some cases, such as the Old Mill site in Mountain View, California, the format became out-dated and complete demolition and redevelopment was appropriate. The old development (above) was adjacent to a healthy regional retail center and a new transit stop.

OPEN SPACE   CIVIC SPACE   EMPLOYMENT   SINGLE-FAMILY   MULTI-FAMILY   COMMERCIAL

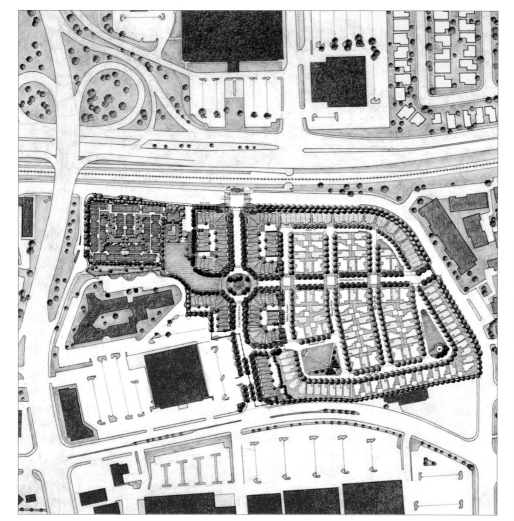

COTTAGES

POCKET PARK

COTTAGE AND TOWNHOMES

[PLATE 29] THE CROSSINGS

MOUNTAIN VIEW, CALIFORNIA

The new neighborhood (above), called The Crossings, provides a range of housing not previously available in the neighborhood. The new housing is complemented by the surrounding office, retail, and single-family homes. At 20 acres it is a small site that could easily have become a gated condominium project. Instead, a series of small city blocks contain a range of housing from small-lot bungalows to high-density townhomes and multistory apartments. Ground-floor shops are located next to the train station, and pocket parks provide gathering places throughout the neighborhood.

▭ = 200 FEET

Part Four: Renewing The Region's Communities

[PLATE 30] UNIVERSITY AVENUE STRATEGIC PLAN
BERKELEY, CALIFORNIA

The strip commercial buildings that line most major arterials are ubiquitous in America. Given the proper zoning, most of these areas could redevelop into mixed-use boulevards. The challenges of creating high-quality places out of these wastelands include the fractured property ownership patterns and the typical shallowness of the properties. The University Avenue Strategic Plan demonstrates that even on a parcel-by-parcel basis (see right middle), such streets can be remade into what can become grand residential boulevards. University Avenue terminates in one of the great Universities of the nation, but it is currently lined by single-story retail, parking lots, and motels. Sections of it have the highest crime rates in the city (see right below). The rezoning allowed denser buildings of up to four floors with retail required at the street level. Along with urban design guidelines, this density bonus is creating significant redevelopment along the Avenue (see far right) and bringing a much-needed residential community to the area.

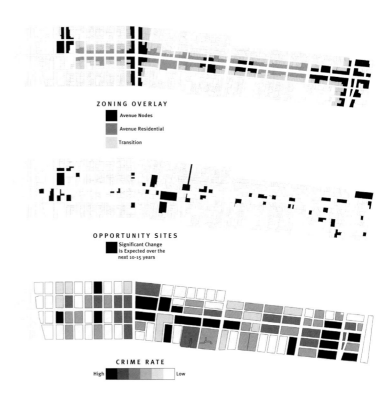

ZONING OVERLAY
- Avenue Nodes
- Avenue Residential
- Transition

OPPORTUNITY SITES
Significant Change is Expected over the next 10-15 years

CRIME RATE
High — Low

HOUSING OVER RETAIL

OPEN SPACE   CIVIC SPACE   EMPLOYMENT   SINGLE-FAMILY   MULTI-FAMILY   COMMERCIAL   ☐ = 200 FEET

[PLATE 31] AGGIE VILLAGE

DAVIS, CALIFORNIA

The character of suburban infill development must relate to the nature and identity of the surrounding community, especially when in a small historic town. The design of Aggie Village reflects the scale and character of the historic fabric of Davis. The tradition of old larger homes set on a grid street pattern is extended into the site and reflected in scale by new duplex dwellings. Each single-family home is architecturally distinct and has a "granny flat" in the rear. A pedestrian way at the center of the project provides access to these cottages.

OPEN SPACE   CIVIC SPACE   EMPLOYMENT   SINGLE-FAMILY   MULTI-FAMILY   COMMERCIAL

= 200 FEET

COTTAGES

DUPLEX

SINGLE-FAMILY

MAIN STREET SHOPS

[PLATE 32] AGGIE VILLAGE
DAVIS, CALIFORNIA

A small retail area is developed around a neighborhood green, preserving a grand old oak tree and placing all the parking to the rear. A café, restaurant, bookstore, and other specialty shops line the arc and are split by a passageway to the parking. Two major stores have front and back door access, an important strategy in providing a more pedestrian-oriented retail configuration. The community green in front of the retail connects the new neighborhood to the surrounding town and forms a gateway to its Main Street.

NEIGHBORHOOD GREEN

Part Four: Renewing The Region's Communities

BEFORE

AFTER

The Suburb's Maturation

SITE PLANS

NORTH ST. PAUL   ☐ = 200 FEET

LAKE ELMO   ☐ = 200 FEET

[PLATE 33] ST. CROIX VALLEY
MINNESOTA AND WISCONSIN

The St. Croix Valley region, which spans the Minnesota–Wisconsin border just east of the Twin Cities, is facing increasing growth and development pressure. Outward development from the Twin Cities region, including major highway improvements, threatens the pre-dominantly rural and small-town character of the Valley, and is placing increasing pressure on the land on and around the St. Croix River. Projections for job and household growth in the St. Croix Valley anticipate an almost 50 percent increase in the number of households by 2020. Citizens in the study area were invited to participate in a regional workshop to solicit input on growth and development issues.

To illustrate the potential for smart growth and walkable development in the study area, six "opportunity sites" on both the Minnesota and Wisconsin sides of the St. Croix River were selected for further study. These are sites or districts with real development potential, spanning a range of conditions, from older downtowns to rural countryside. These three designs (left) show the types of development and infill that could be applied to other communities in the St. Croix Valley. The study helps to show communities how they can develop in ways that are friendly to transit, pedestrians, and the environment and will preserve their community character for coming generations.

NEW RICHMOND   ☐ = 200 FEET

Part Four: Renewing The Region's Communities

[PLATE 34]

MOUNTAIN CORRIDOR SPECIFIC PLAN

ONTARIO, CALIFORNIA

To the northwest of this site was a high-crime housing project, and at the south was a failing power center. The Ontario redevelopment agency sponsored a plan to rebuild this critical gateway to the town. A Main Street, anchored at the top by a major cinema, runs parallel to the arterial and connects the reconfigured power center. Now constructed, the cinema at the head of the Main Street is a clear indication of a trend in entertainment retail toward pedestrian-friendly environments. The housing is to be rebuilt and two gateway parks flank the arterial.

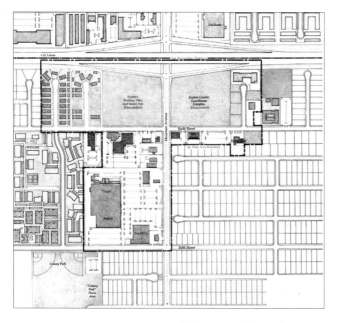

OPEN SPACE   CIVIC SPACE   EMPLOYMENT   SINGLE-FAMILY   MULTI-FAMILY   COMMERCIAL   = 200 FEET

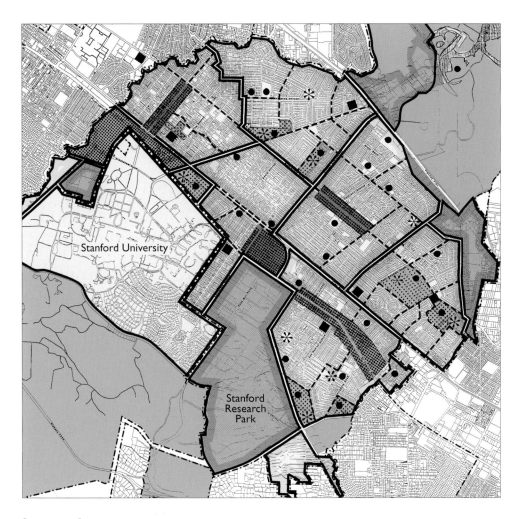

[PLATE 35]

PALO ALTO GENERAL PLAN

PALO ALTO, CALIFORNIA

This small city's General Plan is a clear expression of how to rewrite our planning codes in order to transition from typical isolated single-use designations to increments that support mixed-use place making. The plan shows a framework of walkable neighborhoods, each anchored by commercial centers and public facilities. The dashed lines show the "subneighborhoods" identified by residents in community workshops. In addition to the neighborhood designations, there are three major special districts (including Stanford University and the famous Stanford Research Park) and two mixed-use town-center areas. Finally, the plan shows two "corridors," one human-made along the city's major strip arterial, El Camino Real (now rezoned for mixed-use development), and one natural along the creek at the north edge of the city. This structure of neighborhoods, districts, and corridors forms the framework for a more community-oriented planning system.

TOWN CENTER   MIXED-USE CORRIDOR   NEIGHBORHOOD   EMPLOYMENT   CIVIC SPACE   OPEN SPACE   ✳ = SCHOOLS   ● = PARKS   ☐ = 200 FEET

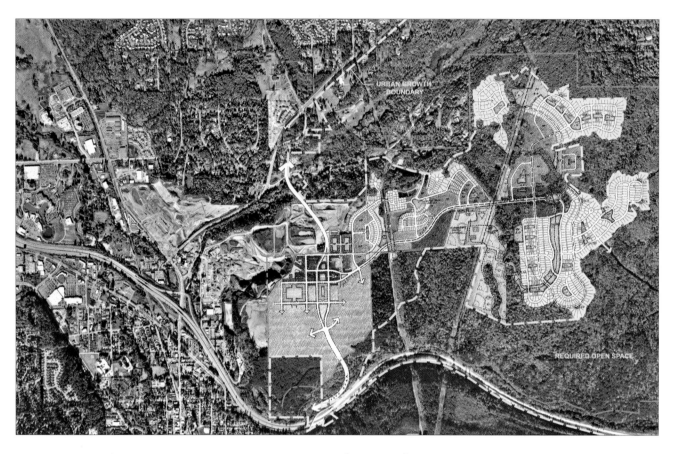

[PLATE 36] ISSAQUAH HIGHLANDS

ISSAQUAH, WASHINGTON

The design for Issaquah Highlands is unique in several ways. It developed a complex open-space system based on natural drainage and aggressive clean-water standards. It was largely the quantity of impervious surfaces that led to the land-use patterns, open-space networks, and designated densities. This new town of approximately 3,200 units also has a very diverse housing program with a high percentage of affordable housing. More important, these affordable units are not segregated into one section of town and will be indistinguishable from the market-rate units.

☐ OPEN SPACE ☐ CIVIC SPACE ☐ EMPLOYMENT ☐ SINGLE-FAMILY ☐ MULTI-FAMILY ☐ COMMERCIAL ☐ = 200 FEET

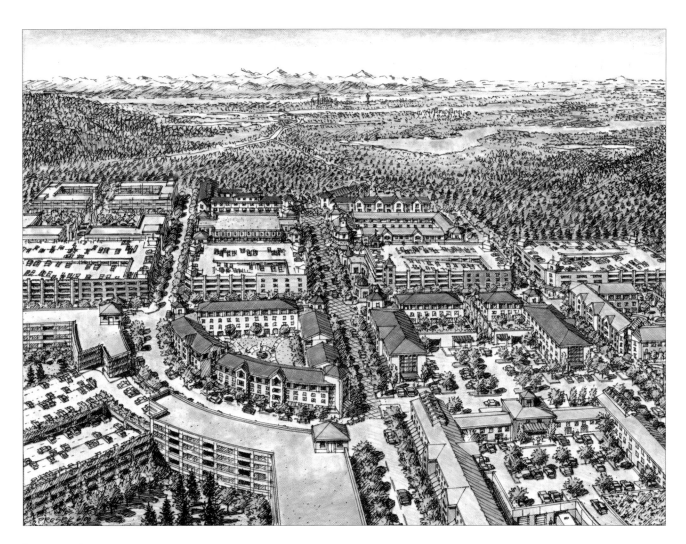

[PLATE 37] ISSAQUAH HIGHLANDS

ISSAQUAH, WASHINGTON

One particularly instructive aspect of the project is the way it deals with a major arterial passing through its town center. The problem of such roads subdividing a town or bypassing them is endemic in many suburbs. At Issaquah the intersecting arterials are split into four one-way streets to form an urban grid. In this way they maintain a pedestrian-friendly dimension and carry similar volumes of traffic. Because of the smaller scale of the one-way streets, the buildings of the town can front directly on the sidewalks and reinforce the urban identity of the place. It is an urban street strategy brought to the suburbs to help in town making.

[PLATE 38] SOUTH EAST ORLANDO SPECIFIC PLAN

ORLANDO, FLORIDA

Covering over 21,000 acres and planning for a population exceeding 80,000 people, the Specific Plan establishes a framework for mixed-use development in the area surrounding Orlando's International Airport. The site's extensive wetlands and habitat were mapped and designated as preserves. Greenbelts were added to these preserved lands to connect them into a continuous open-space network, drainage system, and habitat-protection area. The circulation system, including rail transit, was layered onto this framework. These two networks, natural and circulation, formed the foundation for a series of districts, neighborhood centers, village centers, and town centers. The urban design of each center was controlled by a flexible new planning technique called "block standards." The standards identified four block types that could make up any center: residential, civic, commercial, and, most important, mixed-use. Each type of block was assigned simple standards: a maximum block size, building height limits, maximum parking limits, and, most critical, a minimum amount of "build-to lines" at the perimeter.

TOWN CENTER VILLAGE CENTER NEIGHBORHOOD CENTER EMPLOYMENT GREENWAYS WETLANDS RESIDENTIAL

CHAPTER 10:

RENEWING URBAN NEIGHBORHOODS

Our metropolitan areas cannot become true Regional Cities through the maturation of the suburbs alone. Urban neighborhoods must be transformed as well. As we have pointed out repeatedly in this book, the days when the suburbs can succeed separately from the city are over. The communities in the metropolitan constellation are too deeply intertwined to operate independently of one another. Certainly, urban revitalization, infill, and redevelopment have been prime objectives for most cities for some time. There have been some successes but too many failures. The list of problems is long: racial bias, economic stagnation, gentrification, ossifying bureaucracy, cheap suburban alternatives, deteriorating schools, and red-line appraisals, to name a few. Many strategies for resolving or reducing the magnitude of these constraints are currently in use. But it is clear that these strategies are falling short and that additional means to advance the urban agenda are needed.

Physical design plays a central role in the long-term effectiveness of many efforts to renew urban life, at the same time that essential social and economic programs remain essential. More and more cities are valued for their overall urbanity, rather than singular features. It is not just the new convention center, downtown mall, or a growing central business district that make a city workable in today's economy, it is the simple urbanism of its historic neighborhoods, mixed-use districts, and civic places that sets it apart. Businesses and people in a mobile economy choose location as much for quality of life as for functional assets. Although cities will never compete with suburbs for open-space amenities, parking convenience, and single-family housing opportunities, they can provide the vitality, mix, human scale, history, and excitement that cities traditionally offered—and that are increasingly in demand. To compete, cities must be urban in the best sense, not just dense suburbs.

The disincentives of the city cannot be overcome by urbanism alone; concentrated poverty, poor schools, and a decaying tax base can undermine any urban revitalization effort, no matter how well designed. These primary problems must be addressed at the regional scale as well as locally—they were not created by the city itself and must not become the problems of the city by itself. On the tilted board of today's regional geographies, urban bootstrap efforts are not always enough; they need to be married to a regional vision and a set of regional policies that address affordable housing, schools, and tax-base equity. Given a healthy regional framework, city renewal can successfully reengage the opportunity of traditional urbanism even in the most distressed neighborhoods of the inner city.

The challenge of the city must become the opportunity of the region. As we have stated before, many regional strategies naturally reinforce a movement back to the city. Regional boundaries can make investments in existing communities—even distressed urban neighborhoods—competitive with new growth areas. Regional fair-share housing programs can help deconcentrate the poverty that distorts the culture and future of many inner-city neighborhoods. Regional tax-sharing schemes can rebalance the capacity of cities to provide services and reduce tax burdens on businesses. Regionally targeted school vouchers can make many areas of the city acceptable for middle-class households while empowering lower-income families. And regionally linked transit systems can provide much needed job access for lower-income city residents to the new suburban commercial centers, as well as the reverse. Such regional policies can change the social, economic, and physical chemistry of urban neighborhoods dramatically.

Just as the suburbs are primed for reconfiguration, the possibility of revitalizing many inner-city neighborhoods is emerging in the context of this regional perspective. Under both Secretary Cisneros and Secretary Cuomo, HUD began to understand that the relationship between the city and the region was a two-way street. While regional policies can help the city, the city can help the region overcome sprawl: "HUD supports revitalization efforts and encourages the recognition that many [inner city] communities have untapped markets—labor, purchasing power, and land—which could serve as an alternate to sprawl and fuel the region's economic growth."

Any serious urban revitalization efforts will require rethinking the way in which we approach the long-debated problems and opportunities of the city. Three strategies have emerged as key for HUD and others. First, as has been stated, the opportunities and challenges of urban renewal must be seen in a regional context rather than as problems of an isolated neighborhood, district, or city. Second, the policies, designs, and programs must be conceived as whole systems—whole neighborhoods—rather than isolated programs with separate initiatives. Third, the process to bring about change must be inclusive and from the ground up. Regional design, suburban infill, and urban renewal have these basic strategies in common.

Community participation is as critical to urban revitalization as it is to developing a regional vision. Creating a vision and a way of realizing that vision cannot be a top-down process. The process must simultaneously educate and engage the public as the planners themselves learn from the community. Struggling with the problems is the best way to understand the issues and develop a consensus. The process needs to go well beyond option polls, wish lists, and gripe sessions. It needs to give people the tools to create their own vision and challenge them to formulate their own answers. Community input is rarely enough—simply asking citizens about needs and hopes often feels good but doesn't engage them in creative problem solving. People need hard facts, they need the means to struggle with the problems, and they need to understand the trade-offs of real limits.

In addition to grassroots participation and a new regional perspective, urban revitalization efforts need to be conceived as whole systems. The "social ecology" of a neighborhood needs to be addressed with strategies that unify now disconnected programs, institutions, and policies. The myriad federal and state programs, local city initiatives, local civic groups' efforts, and, most important, neighborhood community group's efforts must be integrated. A unified vision for a neighborhood or urban district that clarifies the connections and possible synergies is at the heart of this type of revitalization effort. All are coupled with a deeper understanding that the physical form of the neighborhood plays a critical role in connecting and facilitating many social and economic programs.

Two federal programs are manifestations of this type of rethinking. First, HUD's Consolidated Planning initiative started in 1993 with the goal of prompting urban districts to develop a neighborhood vision that integrates all the department's programs with local and citywide efforts. The initiative provides the tools, the incentives, and the means for neighborhoods to streamline their applications for support at the same time that they create a unified vision for their future.

Second, HUD's HOPE VI program provides long-needed money to rebuild and redevelop many of the nations worst public housing projects—areas that not only have become tragic crime zones for their inhabitants, but are a drain on surrounding neighborhoods. This program challenges the neighborhood to seek grassroots direction and to think about the larger neighborhood framework while redesigning the public housing projects. It rejects the notion of concentrating subsidized housing by requiring that each rebuilt project integrate housing opportunities for a range of incomes and household types while providing a seamless extension of the historic urban fabric around it.

The federal government is not the only important player in revitalizing urban neighborhoods, and Consolidating Planning and HOPE VI are not panaceas for all urban woes. We focus on these two programs because they target the toughest neighborhoods and represent an acid test for the feasibility of urban revitalization. In these areas, poverty and social decay will not be easily eradicated. Schools, family structure, crime, economic opportunity, and race must all be addressed with new ideas as well as more money—with individual responsibility as well as public commitment. In the next decade, a new alliance of public policy, regional vision, neighborhood consensus, and personal commitment must be forged to rebalance the ecology of our most dysfunctional urban landscapes. HUD's two programs do not provide all the answers. But we believe they contain the seeds of this new alliance.

THE NEIGHBORHOOD AS ECOSYSTEM: HUD'S CONSOLIDATED PLANNING

Ever since the War on Poverty began almost forty years ago, HUD has been deeply involved in urban revitalization through a whole range of programs. Bureaucratic red tape, inefficiency, and even corruption have been the image of HUD programs to many people. Even when programs avoided those pitfalls, they had unintended negative outcomes. The urban-renewal efforts of the 1960s and some public housing projects are good examples of efforts that, even though well intentioned, were ultimately destructive to urban neighborhoods.

In a powerful statement at the beginning of its Consolidated Planning handbook, HUD acknowledged this negative legacy as a first step in redirecting its approach to neighborhood revitalization: "We suggest that the guiding concepts of Consolidated Planning can remedy a long list of past mistakes, including programs that fractured and isolated social services, destroyed community history and identity (both architectural and institutional), isolated income groups, family support systems, and housing types, created "no man's land" open space and buffers, permitted freeways and major roads to dissect neighborhoods and isolate communities, failed to coordinate transit investments with new housing and jobs, dispersed civic facilities and destroyed community focus, displaced small local businesses, and damaged natural systems."

Federal dollars and programs need not corrupt and undermine cities, however. Whether they are helpful depends on the philosophy and the process. In the early 1990s, HUD created the Consolidated Plan process as a way to get both the federal agency and local community groups to think of revitalization as a holistic process. In strictly bureaucratic terms, the purpose of the Consolidated Plan is to combine and consolidate the application process for four federal programs: Community Development Block Grant (CDBG), Home Investment Partnerships (HOME), Housing Opportunities for Persons with AIDS (HOPWA), and Emergency Shelter Grants (ESG).

But the Consolidated Plan also has a broader purpose: to encourage localities to create a broad-ranging neighborhood vision based on extensive community participation. In addition, the Consolidated Plan is meant to look beyond HUD programs and show how other state and federal programs, such as empowerment zones, enterprise zones, and the ISTEA flexible transportation funding, fit into the vision and its implementation. As the HUD handbook points out: "Narrow functional programs cannot solve complex problems of the individual, family, or neighborhood. Our approach must be holistic, linking economic, human, physical, environmental, and design concerns to build viable communities of opportunity."

Community groups were encouraged to look beyond the housing needs generated within the neighborhood to examine strategies that could diversify its population. In many cases, that meant market-rate housing in low-income areas or ownership opportunities in areas dominated by rental housing. As part of their strategic planning, community groups were asked to imagine how the social services in the neighborhood—health, day care, schools, adult education, job training, policing, and civic and religious institutions—could be integrated in ways that would increase efficiencies and strengthen community. And they were asked to look beyond the standard subsidies for economic development to think about regional access to jobs and innovative local business incubators.

In the creation of a Consolidated Plan, the first step is to assess the community assets and needs in a methodical manner, once again looking at the whole picture rather than one dimension at a time. Armed with this overview, a series of community workshops could produce a comprehensive vision for a three- and five-year time frame. This vision, called the Community Partnership Strategy, becomes not only the core of the funding applications to HUD for its once-segregated programs, but also a plan of how all the agencies, community groups, civic institutions, nonprofit organizations, and (most important) individual people and families can coordinate their efforts. Finally, Consolidated Planning calls for the creation of benchmarks to measure progress over time. The benchmarks become a means to keep the vision on track, to provide a self-correcting mechanism and allow the vision to evolve and adapt as it progresses.

Making Connections

The essence of Consolidated Planning is a focus on reestablishing lost connections—connections between people, connections within communities, connections across neighborhoods, cities, and regions, and connections among seemingly unrelated government programs. As HUD's guidebook on Consolidated Plans points out, many of the problems of urban neighborhoods came about when important connections were destroyed, such as community history and identity, physical connections within the neighborhoods, and connections to critical social services and job opportunities.

In laying out how Consolidated Plans might be drawn up, HUD proposed the use of four principles as the foundation. The first, not surprisingly, was "Neighborhood and Community," recognizing that neighborhoods form the foundation of both the community and the region and—as we stated earlier—that many urban neighborhoods have been torn asunder by past urban policies. The other three are similar to the principles that we articulated in Chapter 3:

- *Human development and human scale*—recognizing that individuals and families, not remote institutions, should be the measure of a community

- *Diversity and balance*—recognizing that heterogeneous communities have qualities that can generate the social capital that creates opportunities and growth

- *Sustainability, conservation, and restoration*—recognizing that communities should nurture and restore not only their natural environment, but also their built environment and social fabric

We used these principles previously because we believe they provide a solid foundation for approaching entire communities and regions in a holistic way. For urban neighborhoods in particular, they suggest a very powerful shift in the way that revitalization efforts move forward. With these principles in mind, we can focus on building public programs and economic development strategies around neighborhoods rather than governments. We can replace public housing projects and bureaucratic institutions with human-scale communities and local services. We can advance the idea of diverse communities over functionally isolated government programs and segregated land uses. And we can focus on conserving and restoring human and natural resources rather than squandering them.

In thinking about an urban neighborhood holistically, it's important to understand that all these principles operate on many levels simultaneously. Each applies equally to the social, economic, and physical dimensions of community development.

For example, to apply the principle of *Neighborhood and Community* to all three dimensions—social, economic, and physical—at once requires coordinated efforts that reinforce one another. In relation to this principle, repairing the social fabric might call for a focus on the reclamation of neighborhood institutions, on community policing efforts, on site-based school management, or on building new cultural centers. Economic development might require a focus on strengthening local merchant organizations, on creating community banks, and on determining how jobs in civic and cultural institutions can provide an economic foundation for the neighborhood. The physical-design aspects might require urban design that focuses on reinforcing the neighborhood's civic spaces and supporting safe streets.

Similarly, applying the principle of *Human Development and Human Scale* may mean more policemen walking a beat in social terms; the economic implications may mean supporting small businesses; and the physical implications may be realized in paying greater attention to walkable neighborhoods or in creating buildings with more identity and variation.

When these four principles are applied to all three dimensions, the integrated, well-rounded nature of the Consolidated Plan idea becomes more obvious. Unlike the standard government categories of economic development, housing, education, and health services, the Consolidated Plan attempts to integrate programs and strategies. The idea is to invest in neighborhoods and people, rather than in programs and institutions.

Making Holistic Planning Work

The Consolidated Plan idea is important not because it is a new way to meet federal bureaucratic requirements, but because it illustrates a healthier and more integrated way of examining the problems of urban neighborhoods. Indeed, the consolidated planning philosophy and process would provide a good basis for creating a vision for any neighborhood—urban or suburban—or, indeed, for any region. But, because distressed urban neighborhoods are perhaps the most difficult challenge to the Regional City, holistic thinking is *especially* important in this context.

Since HUD introduced the concept of the Consolidated Plan, many communities throughout the United States have used the ideas therein as a basis for a successful strategy to revitalize urban districts and even entire cities. In some cases, a community's action was stimulated directly by the Consolidated Plan process. In other cases, a community was already attempting to create more integrated plans to revitalize urban neighborhoods and used the Consolidated Plan process as a framework.

The seaside community of Ventura, California, for example, used the Consolidated Plan to create an integrated vision for a low-income and mostly Latino neighborhood—and then used that plan as a guide for how to make the vision a reality.

Ventura is a mostly Anglo, middle-class city. Decades ago, its prosperity depended on oil production around the city's "Westside," one of Ventura's original neighborhoods. In recent decades, however, oil production declined and the Westside was left behind. Although it was a lively and diverse older neighborhood in many ways, the Westside had become largely Latino, mostly poor, and suffered from a lack of attention from the city government.

Working with city funds, a neighborhood association in the Westside neighborhood held a series of public workshops in 1996 at a local elementary school and then presented the City Council with a bottoms-up vision of the neighborhood that focused on urban design, economic development, and revitalization of historic buildings. The centerpiece of the program was the restoration and reuse of the neighborhood's signature building, a handsome brick 1920s "oilman's" hotel.

Federal Community Development Block Grant funds were used to renovate the building. Affordable apartments were created on the top floor, whereas the bottom floor—originally designed for retail shops—provided a new home for the neighborhood's popular community library, which had been located across the street in a rundown minimall for thirty years.

Based on the strength of the Consolidated Plan, the city received a waiver from HUD rules to permit the use of CDBG funds to pay for library operations. The library is now the focal point of the community. It is the most heavily used neighborhood library in the county and the only one where a majority of patrons arrive on foot rather than by car.

The Westside effort received a special "best practices" Consolidated Plan award from HUD, and rightly so. The library project in particular achieved all of the four goals of the Consolidated Plan process. The project focused on *Neighborhood and Community* by working on nuts-and-bolts matters of significance to the Westside neighborhood, including affordable housing and library services. It achieved the goal of *Conservation and Restoration* by renovating the neighborhood's landmark historic building. It focused on *Diversity and Balance* in two ways: by working with the city's most diverse neighborhood and by encouraging a range of uses in close proximity to one another. And it achieved both *Human Development and Human Scale* by providing a library to improve the minds of the community's children that was located within walking distance of most houses and apartments in the neighborhood.

Rochester, New York, has used many of the ideas contained in the Consolidated Plan process to create a whole new neighborhood-oriented vision for the future of the city. Once a leading industrial and corporate center, Rochester is still the home of many important corporate and civic institutions, and it has not suffered from wholesale hollowing out, as many northeastern cities have. Still, the city has suffered from an ongoing decline in population. After peaking at close to 400,000 people four decades ago, Rochester today has only about 200,000 people. And this decline has been accompanied by an increasing concentration of poverty.

Seeking to revitalize the city, Mayor William Johnson created an initiative called Neighbors Building Neighborhoods, or NBN. In the NBN effort, all the city's neighborhoods worked together to create a plan for economic development and renewal, which focused on such nuts-and-bolts matters as cleaning up streetscapes and enforcing city codes more strictly. In 1997, after HUD released its Consolidated Plan guidelines, Rochester undertook a second round of planning—the so-called NBN2 effort, which led to a revision of the city's twenty-five-year-old comprehensive plan. The Renaissance Plan, as it is called, focuses Rochester's efforts on three themes: responsibility (dealing with such matters as education and the environment), opportunity (dealing with economic development), and community (dealing with physical form and a strategy of centers and urban villages).

All these planning efforts have been folded into the city's Consolidated Plan for

HUD, and in fact they form an excellent example of the holistic approach contained in the Consolidated Plan idea. The city's Consolidated Plan serves as the basis for ongoing public involvement in the Community Development Block Grant process, and HUD funds are used for—among other things—preparing an annual monitoring report called Priorities on People. Furthermore, the Renaissance Plan and the Consolidated Plan continue to be used as the basis for implementing the priorities of both the city and the community. For example, when the Rochester United Way decided that six neighborhood centers were in desperate need of renovation, it helped to create a Union Neighborhood Centers Foundation to raise $18 million. The city contributed $1 million in block grant funds under the Consolidated Plan.

However, in keeping with the holistic approach of Consolidated Planning, the city required each neighborhood center to show that it had the support of community residents, including the sector planning group that had written the NBN plan for that geographical area. One old-line neighborhood center that had lost touch with the residents refused to secure the support of its sector planning group—a group known as a the Southwest Common Council, which consisted of five official neighborhood groups. As a result, a new group was soon created—far more representative of the neighborhood—and it now occupies a brand-new community center located on the campus of a new middle school.

Rochester also won a HUD best-practices award. Its combined effort—NBN, the Renaissance Plan, and the Consolidated Plan—also is a realization of the Consolidating Planning idea. Residents in the city's neighborhoods were intimately engaged in setting goals and priorities for their communities—and those ideas were incorporated into the city's overall plan. When it was time to use city financial resources to support true community representation, the Consolidated Plan idea provided the foundation to do it.

These are only two examples of success with the use of the Consolidated Plan; there are dozens more. In Lawrence, Massachusetts, twenty-five miles north of Boston, the city began a "visioning" process after being designated by HUD as an Enterprise Community. The Consolidated Planning process was a joint partnership between the city and Merrimack College, and it has been carried out in conjunction with many community groups, including the Lawrence-Metheun Enterprise Partnership.

In Albuquerque, the city initiated a Consolidated Plan process as a way of using other federal funds to "leverage" the city's designation as an Enterprise Community. The city established a twenty-four-member Citizen Advisory Group to oversee the Consolidated Plan—and, in the second round in 1998, the Consolidated Plan created detailed subarea plans for parts of the region.

In Nashville, the city formed an advisory committee to prepare a Consolidated Plan that included public housing residents, homeless persons, staff from the state community development department, and other people who have traditionally been left out of the process.

Several cities have been recognized for their innovative use of computer mapping to create Consolidated Plans. In Glendale, California, a first-ring suburb of Los Angeles, the Consolidated Plan targeted the business community, social-service providers, and residents of low-income neighborhoods. The result was a joint effort to build a school, park, and community center in which all stakeholders took part.

All these examples represent efforts by distressed neighborhoods to view urban revitalization as a process that requires an integrated vision at the neighborhood level connected to the assets of the surrounding city and region. As stated earlier, it is not the mere fact that HUD encourages Consolidated Planning for the purposes of federal funding that we believe is important. The important point is that the program moves beyond the traditional boundaries of urban revitalization to two fundamental goals: first, to create a vision that, at the neighborhood level, integrates the social, economic, and physical dimensions of community building; and, second, to reinforce connections to the surrounding city and region. In the next section, we will describe one of HUD's most important attempts to carry this idea forward in the nation's most troubled neighborhoods: the HOPE VI public housing program.

REBUILDING THE GHETTO: HUD'S HOPE VI PROGRAM

The federal government's program to rebuild the most troubled public housing in America is an appropriate strategy with which to conclude this book. It is the most challenging test and perhaps the most successful realization of the principles and practices that we have described.

HOPE VI addresses the problems of redevelopment in some of our most economically and socially disadvantaged neighborhoods by rebuilding their decaying public housing projects. It is the ultimate expression of the need as well as the moral obligation to repair and reuse rather than abandon our decaying historic urban neighborhoods. The HOPE VI program demonstrates that our cities, even in their darkest corners, can be revitalized and that we can repair the damage done by misguided urban renewal and housing programs. It shows that we can bring zones once dominated by violence and despair back into the social, economic, and physical fabric of the city. And it proves that economic integration is possible even at the extreme end of our social spectrum.

HOPE VI is replacing more than 60,000 units of the nation's worst public housing in 129 of its toughest neighborhoods. To do so, it has fundamentally rethought the nature and identity of public housing. It calls for public housing to be designed as neighborhoods rather than projects, as housing for many different incomes rather than ghettos for the poor, and as sensitive extensions of a city's urban history rather than the "brave new world" of superblocks and high-rises. In many cases, the housing is razed and the site is reconfigured with a human-scale street pattern and rebuilt with traditional housing forms.

The HOPE VI redevelopment plans design for direct connections to the surrounding neighborhoods, for safe streets, for integrated civic places, and for homes that confer identity and pride. The program supports simple things such as private yards rather than unsafe and ambiguous common areas; street addresses and front porches rather than building numbers and dark halls; and traditional building types and materials rather than modernist apartment blocks. These design shifts create places where each resident, either public housing tenant or working family, share the same residential identity. The visual and functional stigmas of "the projects" are eliminated and replaced with homes, streets, and blocks that fit the character and history of the area. The goal for HOPE VI is always to destigmatize public housing and reconnect it to its surroundings—to make it appear and function as part of the urban neighborhoods that had thrived nearby.

Beyond its physical design, HOPE VI calls for a process of community participation that reconnects public housing occupants not only with nearby neighbors, but also with the larger opportunities in their cities and regions. It asks stakeholders to think about the economic, social, and cultural dimensions of their communities, not just the housing. It challenges them to integrate social services such as health care, day care, security, and after-school programs with job training, local retail, and transportation—to think holistically about their problems and their possibilities.

Just as it goes beyond housing to these social services, Hope VI often goes beyond the boundaries of the "project." Housing authorities are asked to team with tenants, private developers, city officials, and neighborhood groups to develop plans for the public housing site and its surrounding area. The goal is to reestablish a seamless connection to the larger neighborhood and not only repair the discontinuities that the public housing has created, but also address the long-term decay of the entire neighborhood. Off-site infill housing is often used to help repair neighboring blocks and streets—streets that through neglect and proximity to the public housing have often become unsafe and abandoned. This scattered-site housing also serves to further disperse low-income households while it provides more choices for the public housing tenants.

At the heart of HOPE VI is the goal to end poverty's isolation by reconnecting the new housing with its neighbors and by integrating its occupants with market-rate renters and owners. Close to 40 percent of the housing in the program is market rate or subsidized for low-income working households. Home-ownership units are mixed with the rental housing to create a stronger sense of personal investment in the community and provide yet another housing choice. Approximately a quarter of the units provide ownership opportunities, with a third of those going to public housing tenants who are "moving up."

Housing design and construction standards high enough for those with choice have to be met throughout each new development because the public housing units cannot be segregated or differentiated in any way. Mixing affordable and market-rate housing with public housing begins to create a social ladder within the neighborhood. Kids have the kinds of social experiences too often missing in the projects, as new role models live next door and the social standards shift.

To be successful, the new neighborhoods must be supported by high behavioral standards, adequate social services, and reasonable economic opportunities. To this end, the public housing tenants can be screened and, if warranted, they can be evicted. Drug dealing, prostitution, crime, or lack of civil order can be controlled to everyone's benefit. In the few instances when the screening and standards could not be enforced, the viability of the neighborhood as a mixed-income area suffered.

In some cases, the combination of adding the affordable and market-rate units along with building at an appropriate (but lower) density means that all the public housing is not replaced on-site. However, in all cases, scattered-site housing or rental vouchers are made available to the public housing tenants to make up the difference. Close to a third of the 60,000 units scheduled for demolition are unoccupied. Approximately 38,000 new or rehabilitated public housing units have been built or are under construction, along with 24,000 additional units for working and mixed-income families. The gap for public housing tenants has been filled with 15,000 Section 8 rental vouchers. For some, an opportunity to leave the project area is attractive, an opportunity to make a new life in a new place. Many others choose to stay in the community that they know and return to one of the new housing units.

In sum, the goals of HOPE VI are complex. They are to create mixed-income neighborhoods in the place of projects; to rebuild public housing to fit an area's history and surrounding character; to support self-sufficiency and independence through a continuum of social and economic programs; and to promote private- and public-sector partnerships to leverage public investments and increase economic development. These are honorable goals that are now being achieved. A sampling of the kinds of results that HOPE VI has created follows.

Centennial Place, Atlanta

Over the past five years, Centennial Place in Atlanta has become one of the HOPE VI program's showcases. In Centennial Place, the reconstruction of a major public housing complex has succeeded in deconcentrating poverty, restoring a sense of community, and creating a focal point for a holistic and integrated mixed-income revival of an important inner-city neighborhood in Atlanta.

Located adjacent to the campus of the Georgia Institute of Technology, Techwood Homes was the first public housing project ever constructed in the United States. As part of the original, New Deal–era federal public housing program, it was originally aimed at white working-class families, most of whom could not afford adequate housing during the Great Depression. At the Techwood Homes dedication, on the day after Thanksgiving 1935, President Franklin Roosevelt declared: "Here, at the request of the citizens of Atlanta, we have cleaned out nine square blocks of antiquated squalid dwellings, for years a detriment to this community. Today those hopeless old houses are gone and in their place we see the bright cheerful buildings of the Techwood Housing Project."

A half century later, Techwood Homes had deteriorated into a typical public housing project, characterized by racial segregation (mostly black), an extreme concentration of poverty, and a rapid physical deterioration. The Techwood neighborhood (which included the adjacent Clark Howell public housing project) is located not far from downtown Atlanta, bounded on the north by Georgia Tech and on the south by the corporate headquarters of Coca-Cola, one of the nation's most successful companies. Yet the Techwood neighborhood was so empty of life that it was known locally as "The Void." The Atlanta Housing Authority, which ran the facility, was considered one of the most poorly run public housing authorities in the nation as recently as 1993. Citywide, several thousand units of public housing were boarded up and vacant.

As Atlanta prepared for the 1996 Summer Olympics, however, local officials decided to use the opportunity to create a dramatic turnaround of its public housing projects, focusing first on the Clark-Techwood neighborhood. In 1995, HUD provided the Atlanta Housing Authority with a $42.5 million HOPE VI grant.

In a remarkable turnaround, the Housing Authority then pieced together another $160 million in public and private financing to create the first mixed-income project under HOPE VI and the first major partnership with private developers. Other than the HOPE VI grant, all of the rest of the money came from private investors. Most of the funding came from a private development company, The Integral Group. The rest came from investors taking advantage of the federal Low Income Housing Tax Credit program, which provides investors with tax credits for investing in affordable housing projects.

The Housing Authority razed almost 1,100 units of public housing in the Clark and Techwood projects. On the 57-acre site once occupied by these projects, the Housing Authority constructed Centennial Place, a 900-unit mixed-income project that has served as the centerpiece for the revitalization of an entire neighborhood.

Centennial Place itself has become a testament to the success of the mixed-income concept. Under the agreement among HUD, the Housing Authority, and private developers, 360 units in Centennial Place (40 percent) are traditional public housing units. Another 180 units (20 percent) are available to low- and moderate-income residents under the federal Low Income Housing Tax Credit program. The final 360 units (40 percent) are market-rate units renting for between $500 and $900 per month.

The current group of residents is a remarkable mixture. The people who currently live there relocated from some seventy different zip codes in the Atlanta area. Almost half of all residents have incomes greater than $35,000 per year, whereas one in five has an income greater than $55,000 per year. At the same time, Centennial Place remains home to many extremely poor and working-poor families. Their own sense of identity was so dramatically altered that the tenants changed the name of the Tenants' Association to the Residents' Association.

Importantly, however, the Centennial Place project is not a single-use project focused on housing. It serves as the centerpiece for an entire neighborhood revitalization effort that has taken advantage of the project's location and its proximity to Georgia Tech. The project also includes a new YMCA, a branch bank, a Holiday Inn Express Hotel, a bicycle police patrol substation, and a day-care center. A library dating from 1909 and a community center dating from 1941 have been renovated. The project has been designated as a "Campus of Learners." It includes a new elementary school with an innovative technology-based curriculum designed in collaboration with Georgia Tech (with which the school has special computer connections).

The local Workforce Enterprise Program provides job and computer training in the neighborhood for Centennial Place residents, who also receive state-of-the-art computer wiring in their apartments. Many of these services are provided by a partnership between the Atlanta Housing Authority and three historically black colleges. But perhaps most important is the fact that the traditional public housing residents cannot simply draw on Centennial Place as an entitlement indefinitely. They must be working part time or participate in a work-training program to continue to live there.

The Terraces, Baltimore

Few American cities suffer from such extreme concentrations of poverty and regional imbalances as Baltimore. In general, the Baltimore-Washington metropolitan area is one of the richest and fastest-growing in the nation. In downtown Baltimore, decades of careful urban revitalization planning have finally paid off, as the Inner Harbor area has emerged as a strongly revitalized business and tourist environment. The rest of the city of Baltimore, however, has suffered from an extreme cycle of white flight, racial segregation, concentrated poverty, and lack of investment.

From the beginning of the HOPE VI project, Baltimore has been an important participant in the program, securing grants for the renovation of several projects. One of the most successful has been The Terraces, a mixed-income and mixed-tenure project constructed on the site of the former Lexington Terrace public housing project.

Lexington Terrace was a typical 1950s high-rise public housing project built in West Baltimore, where a group of public housing projects have created an extreme concentration of poverty. With a $22 million HOPE VI grant, the Housing Authority of Baltimore undertook a $45 million plan to create 303 new housing units—including 100 townhomes for sale. As with Centennial Place, The Terraces included a partnership between the Housing Authority and private developers, as well as private financing—in this case, some $10 million from NationsBank (now Bank of America), the nation's largest bank.

The for-sale townhomes were priced at between $43,000 and $65,000, and half were set aside for families with annual incomes of less than $27,000—thus making home ownership possible for the first time for many working-poor families. The buyers were required to make a down payment of only $1,000 and they received a favorable interest rate of 6.6 percent. Many of the buyers were working-poor families that had never before lived outside of the projects.

As at Centennial Place, however, the real success of The Terraces lies in more than just the housing project itself. Other aspects of The Terraces project seek to connect its residents to a broader economy, which simply did not exist in West Baltimore before HOPE VI. The Terraces project includes what local officials call "an e-village," where project residents can obtain as much as two weeks of free computer training; they also obtain computers at no cost or buy them at a greatly reduced rate. The Terraces includes the first combination business and retail center (including a Rite Aid pharmacy) contained within a HOPE VI project.

To people who live in the suburbs, it may seem odd that the developers of a "housing project" place such high priority on access to computers, to jobs, and to a pharmacy. But these are exactly the types of community-building activities that have been lacking in inner-city neighborhoods. By introducing them into West Baltimore and elsewhere, HOPE VI has helped to restore the community fabric that was torn asunder decades ago when high-rise public housing projects were built.

These community services are especially important in places like West Baltimore, where several public housing projects stand in close proximity to one another, thus creating an extreme concentration of poverty. Several other HOPE VI projects are moving forward in West Baltimore, and together they hold the potential to break the concentration of poverty and restore a sense of community.

First Ward Place, Charlotte

Like so many other American cities, Charlotte, North Carolina, has a concentration of poverty and public housing that sprung up on the outskirts of its downtown as the result of several generations of urban-renewal efforts. The First Ward Place project is an attempt to use HOPE VI to restore a true community in a desolate area that was once one of the city's most vibrant and integrated neighborhoods.

Once a city of handsome and diverse neighborhoods surrounding the downtown, Charlotte was especially hard hit by the federal bulldozer. In the 1950s, the city's urban-renewal program razed the Brooklyn neighborhood, a mostly black neighborhood that contained some of the city's worst slums. More than a thousand families were displaced, but the land was sold off mostly to office developers and not a single residential unit was replaced.

Under pressure from the federal government to build replacement housing, Charlotte then razed the black residential core of the First Ward. According to Charlotte historian Thomas Hanchette, the First Ward had historically been a neighborhood that was integrated both racially and economically. On some streets, whites and blacks lived side by side all through the Jim Crow era, and whites did not leave the First Ward until urban renewal in Brooklyn led to a huge increase in housing demand by displaced black families. After a part of the First Ward was razed, the old neighborhood was replaced by Earle Village, a 400-unit low-rise public housing development.

Although Earle Village received great acclaim for its design, it did not alleviate pressure for housing. And, over time, it became a classic center of poverty. In the 1970s, the rest of the First Ward surrounding Earle Village also was cleared, leaving this once-proud district bereft of community. In 1994 alone, more than 700 crimes, including two murders, were committed in the area.

Under HOPE VI, the Charlotte Housing Authority and NationsBank began working together to revitalize the First Ward. (NationsBank's corporate headquarters is located only a few blocks away.) Using a $41 million HOPE VI grant as the foundation, the Housing Authority and NationsBank Community Development demolished Earle

Village, replacing it with First Ward Place, a mixed-income housing project with almost the same number of units.

As with other HOPE VI projects, First Ward Place is a mixture not only of incomes but also of housing types. It includes 282 rental units, 68 senior apartments, 17 for-sale single-family units, and 6 for-sale townhouses. As with Atlanta's Centennial Place (which served as a model for the project), First Ward Place is 40 percent market-rate units, 40 percent traditional public housing units, and 20 percent units for the working poor eligible under the Low Income Housing Tax Credit program. The project has drawn many suburbanites looking for proximity to their downtown jobs, and crime has dropped dramatically. In 1997, in First Ward Place 88 crimes were committed but no murders, a drop of almost 90 percent from only three years before.

The Housing Authority and Bank of America are now building on the First Ward Place success, both in the First Ward and elsewhere in Charlotte. Two other HOPE VI projects are underway in Charlotte, and other projects are moving forward in the mostly vacant First Ward. An Episcopal church is constructing a school in the First Ward, and Bank of America is moving forward with a project to build 80 single-family homes and more than 100 condominium projects—all market rate—on an adjacent plot of land.

Conclusion

Impressive as the HOPE VI and the Consolidated Plan success stories are on their own, it is important to place them in the context of the Regional City concept as a whole. As we have stated from the beginning of this book, the Regional City cannot thrive unless all of its neighborhoods thrive as diverse and vibrant places. HOPE VI is an important step in transforming our poorest and toughest urban neighborhoods into strong communities that play an important role in the city and region. It has provided an opportunity for the federal government, local governments, local institutions, tenants, local citizens, and private businesses such as developers and retailers to work together to repair the long-damaged fabric of inner-city neighborhoods.

Yet just as it is wrong to view inner-city revitalization as a separate problem from regional problems of sprawl and inequity, it is wrong to view even the successes of HOPE VI as an isolated exercise only in inner-city revitalization. HOPE VI is only one tool—albeit an important one—in transforming our metropolitan areas; it must be seen as part of a larger program partly defined by Consolidated Planning and partly defined by the larger regional programs for tax equity, fair-share affordable housing, and economic development.

HOPE VI has been criticized by some as simply another attempt to remove low-income people from neighborhoods now viewed as desirable by developers, business interests, and the upper-middle class. This criticism is derived mostly from the fact that, by reducing densities and mixing incomes, HOPE VI has reduced the number of housing units available to low-income people in the neighborhoods where they have historically lived. These critics simply do not believe that the low-income units will be replaced elsewhere in the metropolis, and therefore poor people will "lose out" yet again in an urban-revitalization effort supposedly designed to help them.

Given the dismal record of urban renewal in this country—as revealed especially in the Charlotte experience—this skepticism is perfectly understandable. That is why successes such as HOPE VI cannot be pursued by themselves but, rather, must be pursued as part of a regional approach. In the past, urban-revitalization efforts failed because they focused simply on housing the poor in poor neighborhoods, rather than creating healthy and diverse neighborhoods throughout a region. The result has been a greater concentration of poverty than ever before and therefore a greater metropolitan inequity than ever before.

That is why HOPE VI must be married to all the other federal, city, regional, and local efforts. Section 8 vouchers and other regional housing initiatives, such as the inclusionary housing requirements of New Jersey and Montgomery County, Maryland, must provide housing opportunity for people of all income groups throughout the Regional City. Transportation and land use policies must be altered to provide more locational and mobility choices for poor people who have little choice (and for middle-class people chained to their automobiles). Private investors must be motivated to look at all neighborhoods and districts in the region, not just the "favored quarter." Choices for jobs and education must be as attractive throughout the region—including inner-city neighborhoods—as they are in affluent suburbs.

By themselves, HOPE VI and all the other innovative and exciting efforts that have emerged in the past ten years will make marginal improvements in our metropolitan neighborhoods. But, by working together on a regional basis, they can become much more powerful. They can create—and bring about—a new vision of the Regional City, one in which the twin problems of sprawl and inequity can at last be attacked at their roots.

URBAN REVITALIZATION

HENRY HORNER HOUSING — BEFORE AND AFTER

[PLATE 39]

Urban revitalization takes many forms in differing circumstances. This section highlights infill in urban neighborhoods with an emphasis on the Department of Housing and Urban Development (HUD) HOPE VI—a program designed to rebuild the most distressed public housing in the country. The underlying principles of this program match all well-conceived infill and redevelopment plans: the area must be seen as part of a neighborhood rather than an isolated "project," it must be diverse in population and uses, it must make a seamless connection to the surrounding community and the urban history of the area, and it must integrate social programs, economic development, and urban design. In all cases the replacement housing achieves a diverse population by mixing affordable housing with market rate units. The results of the effort have been significant. HOPE VI is replacing over 60,000 units of the nation's worst public housing in 124 of its toughest neighborhoods. Areas around the redevelopments have seen drops in crime rates of up to 72 percent. All of the HOPE VI projects illustrated here have been awarded funding in a competitive process by HUD and construction is underway on some.

Shown at left is the transformation of the Henry Horner homes in Chicago. The midrise apartments had become dysfunctional dwellings of high crime, high maintenance costs, and social isolation. The replacement housing reestablished the historic block scale with the mixed-income housing that had once helped make the neighborhood a strong community.

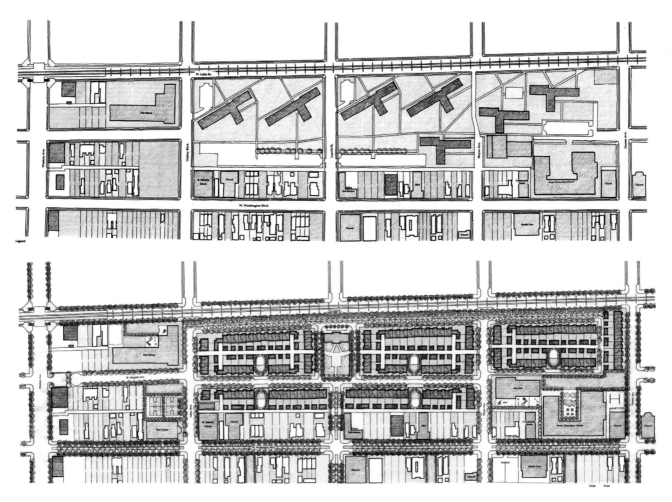

[PLATE 40] HENRY HORNER HOUSING
CHICAGO, ILLINOIS

The old site plan for Henry Horner Housing (top) clearly shows the discontinuity between the historic urban fabric and the isolated midrise apartments. The areas immediately surrounding the housing were very vulnerable to crime, as is the case in many public housing projects. Yet the assets of the site are plentiful: an abundance of schools, churches, and civic uses surround the housing, transit runs just to the north, and a commercial street is within walking distance. As the preliminary plan for replacement housing (bottom) reestablished the tradition of street-front townhomes, stoops, and private yards, the once-dangerous surroundings were eliminated and safe connections to the neighborhood were reestablished. As a result, there has been significant new private investment in housing and commercial development in an area that once was home to empty lots, burned-out houses, and failing stores.

□▬▬▬ = 200 FEET

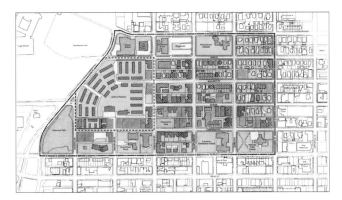

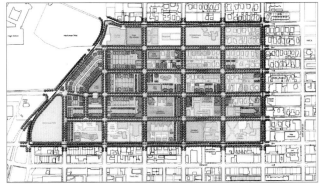

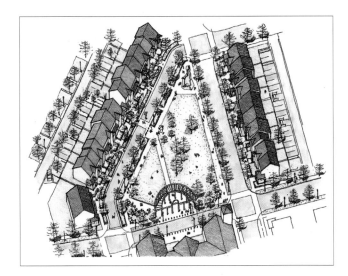

[PLATE 41] CHURCHILL NEIGHBORHOOD
HOLYOKE, MASSACHUSETTS

This HOPE VI redevelopment is a significant example of leveraging the HUD program to repair and revitalize a complete neighborhood rather than just a public housing site (in this case, the Jackson Parkway). The new site plan indicates the many infill and rehabilitation sites throughout the surrounding neighborhood. Much of the worst crime and urban decay was actually located in the blocks just to the east of the public housing, in vacant tenement buildings and empty lots. The plan calls for 120 new units off-site to complement 110 on-site. The mix of market rate affordable to public housing units is equal. Within the public housing site, the open space, too large and lacking in natural surveillance, has been reconfigured into a more compact form with townhomes and a new community center lining its edges. In addition to the housing, the project will develop a "Campus of Learning" to include job training, access to emerging technology, and an array of classes.

OPEN SPACE CIVIC SPACE EMPLOYMENT SINGLE-FAMILY MULTI-FAMILY COMMERCIAL ☐ = 200 FEET

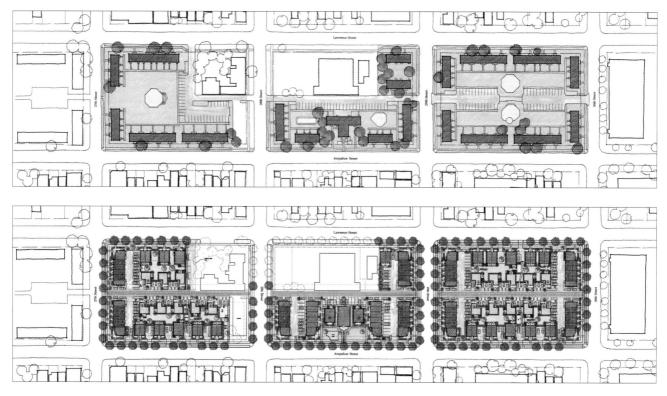

[PLATE 42] CURTIS PARK

DENVER, COLORADO

Curtis Park is a historic mixed-use neighborhood of single-family homes and townhomes just to the east of downtown Denver. The public housing in the neighborhood, though well maintained, did not reflect the economic diversity or urban quality of its surrounding community. On this site, the city's block pattern was still intact but the identity and character of the barrack-like buildings stigmatized the public housing residents. The redevelopment plan sets duplex homes along the long street fronts. These are designed to reflect the character of the older, larger single-family residences of the neighborhood (bottom rendering). In a reinterpretation of the historic standard, the alleyways are lined with one-bedroom cottages (middle rendering) making the alley into more of a residential lane. The ends of the blocks are lined with live/work townhomes—picking up on the mixed-use nature of the neighborhood. This live/work component acknowledges the growing work-at-home needs of many struggling households.

= 200 FEET

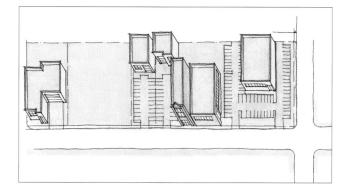

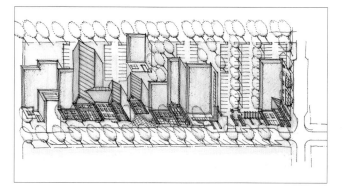

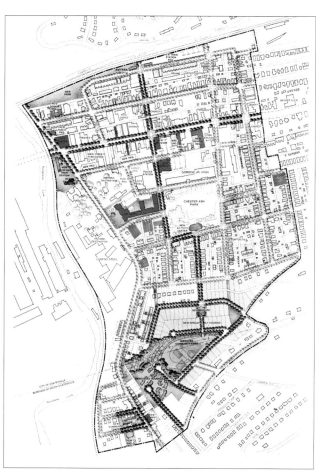

[PLATE 43] OAK STREET REVITALIZATION PLAN
COATESVILLE, PENNSYLVANIA

Coatesville is an old industrial town with a concrete block of public housing perched on a hill overlooking the center of the community. The revitalization plan replaces the apartment block with a large community park at the top of the hill and new single-family homes just below. There is extensive scattered site infill and rehabilitation throughout the study area that extends all the way down to the historic Main Street of the town. In fact, part of the HUD redevelopment is used to help revitalize this Main Street (above left) by infilling several parcels with senior housing and new commercial development. This is another example of HOPE VI working to repair and enhance a whole neighborhood and not just a public housing site.

EXISTING PUBLIC HOUSING

| ■ OPEN SPACE | ▨ CIVIC SPACE | ▨ EMPLOYMENT | □ SINGLE-FAMILY | ▨ MULTI-FAMILY | ▨ COMMERCIAL | □ = 200 FEET |

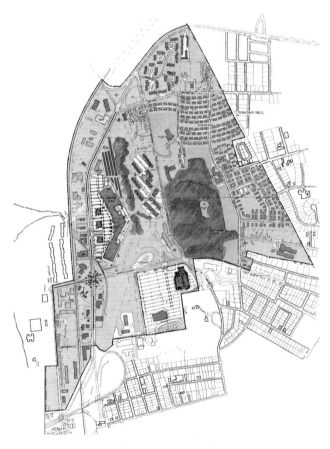

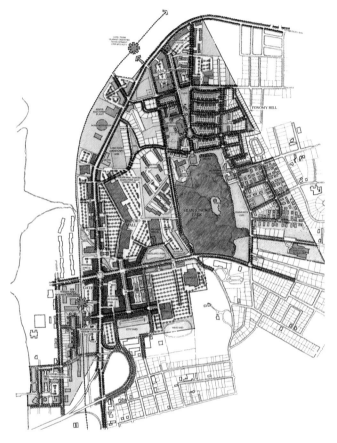

[PLATE 44] NORTH END MASTER PLAN
NEWPORT, RHODE ISLAND

Newport is famous as a wealthy sailor's paradise. Many of our country's finest examples of turn-of-the-century mansion architecture are located there. Few realize that its north end contains an isolated and distressed public housing complex. The city, in collaboration with the Public Housing Authority, requested an area plan that combined the rebuilding of the housing with a redevelopment plan for the strip commercial area just to the north of the town's main entrance. The plan that resulted from extensive community workshops brought together citizens from all parts of the town and shows a mixed-use development of the pubic housing site and a Main Street redevelopment of the old comercial areas.

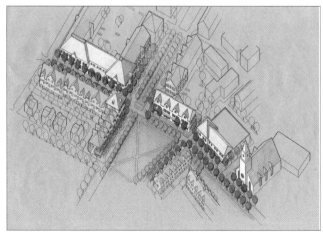

OPEN SPACE　　CIVIC SPACE　　EMPLOYMENT　　SINGLE-FAMILY　　MULTI-FAMILY　　COMMERCIAL　　☐ = 200 FEET

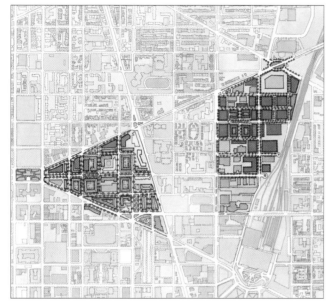

[PLATE 45]

NORTH OF MASSACHUSETTS AVENUE PLAN (NoMa)

WASHINGTON, D.C.

This study of a major area just to the north of Union Station was inspired by the planned construction of the city's new convention center and the surrounding development it would generate. The two areas of the study had differing goals: in the Mt. Vernon Triangle to the west (shown before/after below), the goal was to create a mixed-use area with an emphasis on housing. In the North Capital Avenue area (shown before/after at bottom), the goal was to diversify the city's economy by creating a mixed-use area that could become an incubator for emerging technology companies. Both goals show an effort to diversify the center of the Capital with uses atypical to a district long dominated by large office buildings.

 = 200 FEET

[PLATE 46] NORTH OF MASSACHUSETTS AVENUE PLAN (NoMa)

WASHINGTON, D.C.

The city and neighborhood groups recognized the value of mixed-use urban environments, the need to preserve an existing arts community, and the need to diversify the economy of the city. Along with programs to support housing and the high-tech industries now missing from the economic mix of the downtown area, were urban design controls to allow lofts in converted warehouses and artist studios in surrounding infill locations. Shown in the before and after overview above, the gateway treatment of New York Avenue as it enters the central city is enhanced by the traditional traffic circle so unique to Washington and L'Enfant's plan. The structure of his famous radial boulevards is reinforced with new and rehabilitated buildings that orient to the streets.

CONCLUSION:

TRANSFORMING THE EDGE CITY INTO THE REGIONAL CITY

The real-world task of transforming our metropolitan regions into Regional Cities is not an easy one. This is so not because the concept is hard to grasp or because the tools that we need are unavailable, but because the special interests aligned against the Regional City are many and the bureaucratic bias is institutionalized. In the real world, vested interests and inertia often block needed change. The list of special interests that believe sprawl benefits them is virtually endless. Many developers, builders, engineers, and contractors want the chance to repeat past successes, despite changing times and untold consequences. Many local governments look for growth and an expanded tax base without regard for development quality or regional implications. Neighborhood groups and homeowner associations hope to enhance property values by exclusionary practices. Even environmental groups sometimes promote sprawl by encouraging low-density development or no development at all, at least in the localities where they operate.

Not surprisingly, the advocates of suburban "business as usual" bring with them a series of strong and seemingly persuasive arguments in favor of sprawl and against the Regional City. In strident fashion, they make four major pro-sprawl arguments. First, they say, land in America is plentiful. Urban growth takes up less than 5 percent of the nation's entire land area, and even if we preserve environmentally sensitive areas, there is more than enough land to sprawl as we like. Second, they claim, we can solve the problems created by sprawl simply by building more roads. Automobiles are a truly democratic form of transportation, allowing ordinary people to travel when and where they wish. Because most people drive most places, they claim, the answer is simply to provide them with more roads. If access to these roads must be restricted, it should be restricted by "congestion pricing"—the idea that people should pay a premium to drive on highways at peak periods. Third, the pro-sprawl advocates argue that everybody wants to live in a detached single-family house in the suburbs. Traditional suburban subdivisions, like additional road capacity, simply give people what they want. Finally, the argument goes, private-property rights should be respected.

People should be able to do what they want with their property without intrusive interference from government agencies engaged in regional planning.

There is some truth in each of these statements. In the aggregate, land is plentiful in America. Most people will probably continue to drive most places, and we must pay attention to maintaining and using our roads well. Many people prefer to live in detached single-family homes. And the rights of property owners must always be respected when dealing with matters of land use and land development.

Even though each point is partly true, all four of them miss the larger point about ending sprawl and transforming our metropolitan areas into Regional Cities. And, as the larger truths in each of these areas emerge, they are helping to lay the groundwork for a new coalition capable of overcoming the vested interests and helping to make the Regional City a reality.

Yes, land in America is still plentiful in the aggregate. But this simplistic quantitative statement overlooks the qualitative problems that most citizens confront every day. The fact that vast tracts of land might be available thousands of miles away in rural America matters little to the dwellers of today's growing metropolis. In the areas of greatest population growth, America's coastal areas, 53 percent of the population is jamming into only 17 percent of our nation's land area. Regions require well-functioning natural systems and open-space networks in the areas where growth and change is taking place, not far away. Such open-space networks also can serve to maintain local agricultural production, provide a framework for metropolitan form, and give those who live in metropolitan areas a respite from the asphalt that dominates their daily lives.

Similarly, it is theoretically possible to alleviate traffic congestion temporarily by building more roads, but, again, this begs the question of how to get ahead of the growth curve. More roads lead inevitably to more auto-oriented development and therefore more congestion. As traffic engineer Walter Kulash has said, "Adding roads to cure congestion is a little like loosening one's belt to cure obesity."

Perhaps the most erroneous notion among all of these arguments is that most people "want" to live in low-density, single-family subdivisions and that regional planning will frustrate this "natural" market for single-family homes. In fact, the market is far more diverse than this antiquated view would suggest, and most often local zoning codes—not regional planning—frustrate the market by reducing the choices available.

As we have stated before, only a quarter of all American households consist of families with children at home. Yet many communities now practice exclusionary zoning by allowing only large-lot homes to be built in their jurisdictions, thus excluding housing that meets the needs of many nonfamily households and seniors. It's true that many consumers seem to prefer single-family homes, but often that apparent preference is due to a lack of significant choices. In a market constrained by zoning to single-family subdivisions, isolated apartment complexes, or age-restricted condos, it is no wonder that single-family housing is preferred. If there were more choices, such as bungalows in walkable villages, townhomes in real towns, or lofts and apartments in exciting cities, the housing market would reflect more diversity. Indeed, in cases when such choices are available, they almost always outperform the overall real estate market.

The private-property rights argument has also grown in popularity in recent years, as property owners and ideologically committed property-rights lawyers have sought to reduce the power of government to restrict the use of land. But, at the same time, it has become increasingly clear that individual property owners, no less than welfare mothers, have responsibilities as well as rights. Planning has always been a way of balancing individual rights with community needs. To operate in a metropolitan environment, any property owner requires highways, roads, sewers, water systems, and other public services that will be provided at least in part from tax revenue. It is a defensible and conservative policy to seek out and implement the most cost-effective set of public investments to support growth, as Maryland's Smart Growth laws have done.

The apologists for sprawl always seem to resort to oversimplifications and stereotypes that sidestep the challenge of finding new forms that expand choices. What if we could conserve accessible open space and provide a full range of housing options? What if we expanded the flexibility of the car by adding the choice to walk, bike, or use transit? What if people had choices more expansive than gridlocked suburbs or crime-ridden cities? What if we began to define a new metropolitan form—one that was not black or white, car or train, high density or low, suburban or urban? What if we got past the rhetorical extremes and set to work designing complex, multifaceted communities that fit the postindustrial society that we are becoming.

The American Dream is changing. The future is not necessarily a linear extension of the past, and yesterday's market is not necessarily tomorrow's. The issue is not density but design, the quality of place, its scale, mix, and connections. The alternative to sprawl is not a forced march back to the city but a hierarchy of places—each walkable and diverse—of various densities and in various locations.

The real challenges are quite different from those articulated by the advocates of sprawl. They are the tough choices and difficult political trade-offs that set a course for fundamentally different futures. Where and how much greenfield development is appropriate? Which transportation investments are best? How do we overcome local opposition to infill and redevelopment, and how do we prevent gentrification when such development becomes overly successful? How do we redirect job growth and investment into communities that need it the most? How do we ensure a sufficient supply of affordable housing and its appropriate location? These are some of the difficult questions that must be answered by a regional vision and a new model of development at the neighborhood scale.

History teaches us that when circumstances become ripe enough—and choices for the future become clear—it is possible to overcome vested interests or even bring them together in new coalitions. In the past few years, even as many vested interests have continued to battle in favor of the status quo, we have begun to see new coalitions arise in support of the Regional City and the ideas that underlie it as a concept.

This new set of coalitions goes by many names and represents many groups. Most often, it is called Smart Growth—a recognition that the question today is not whether growth occurs, but how. The New Urbanism is clearly at the heart of this movement, as are concepts such as "Sustainability," "Livable Communities," and "Metropolitanism." Whatever it is called, we believe that this movement is an important breakthrough in overcoming the institutional inertia and vested interests supporting sprawl and inequity.

Independently, many special-interest groups are joining this movement. Some environmental groups and developer institutions such as the Urban Land Institute (ULI) have embraced the concept of Smart Growth. Inner-city advocates have begun to recognize the regional context as a necessary part of their strategies. Inner-ring suburbs have begun to recognize that they have much in common with older urban areas. Many business leaders have come to see affordable housing and long-distance commuting as real workforce problems, and, after a half century of suburban growth, some developers have begun to value infill opportunities in city neighborhoods and maturing suburbs.

Beyond the organized groups is a general sense by the public at large that change must come. A recent national poll by the Pew Center on Civic Journalism showed that concerns about sprawl were now edging out the more traditional local issues such as education and crime. Surprisingly, those polled seemed to have the answer as well as the worry; of all respondents, 40 percent agreed that "local government should try to limit growth in less-developed areas and encourage growth only in areas that are already built up."

As this movement gathers momentum, new alliances are forming. By thinking broadly, a large range of constituencies—forward-thinking environmentalists, enlightened commercial interests, inner-city advocates, thoughtful elected officials— are finding common purpose. Regional City strategies unify environmentalists for open space with inner-city advocates for economic development. They link developers interested in infill projects with environmentalists seeking to increase transit use and reduce auto pollution. They help elected officials in inner cities and older suburbs work together to revive their communities. Even political partisanship is often left behind in these new alliances. At the state level, Democratic Governor Parris Glendening of Maryland and Republican Governor Christie Todd Whitman of New Jersey have often stood ideologically side by side to advocate for a change in our approach to metropolitan growth

As the movement toward the Regional City gains strength, it is important to remember its most basic tenets. They are the summation of three important trends in metropolitan growth that we identified at the beginning of this book—the emergence of the region, the maturation of the suburbs, and the revival of urban neighborhoods. Its direction is set by goals that are in some cases very simple and measurable: to save land, to reduce the need for cars, to use investments efficiently, to conserve resources, and to reduce pollution. In other cases, its goals are complex and immeasurable: to create more inclusive human habitats; to foster connections across age, income, and class; to support social equity and opportunity; and to create beauty in the human-made environment.

But its realization cannot be achieved on a piecemeal basis; nor can it be successful if it operates entirely "inside the box" of the local jurisdictions and the weak-kneed regional policy frameworks that have been used in the past two generations. For example, urban-revitalization strategies are not likely to succeed in the absence of a regional strategy to combat sprawl and inequity—because we cannot truly overcome urban decay if the poor continue to be concentrated largely in urban neighborhoods. Similarly, the reshaping of older suburbs cannot take place in a vacuum. Efforts to reduce auto dependency everywhere and reduce environmental destruction on the fringe cannot succeed unless they are tied to regional transportation and open-space strategies and a new design ethic at the scale of neighborhoods. And the region—even if it is the basic economic unit in the global economy—cannot thrive unless it is consciously designed with strong physical and economic connections between the city, suburb, and countryside.

In other words, we cannot treat these different aspects of metropolitan life—poverty, inequity, sprawl, traffic congestion, loss of open space, and so forth—as if they are separate problems. We must weave them together into a cohesive whole that recognizes both the region and the neighborhood as the building blocks of our daily life.

Throughout this book, we have argued that America is changing—that sprawl no longer fits our population, our demographics, or our economy and that most of our nation would be better off with a new approach. What is remarkable about the movement that has emerged is that it shows a growing awareness across the board—among special-interest groups, politicians, businesses, and average people—that more of the same will not work.

The Regional City is not a utopian construct. Although it projects a future that is quite different from what would emerge from present trends, it does not assume that we must start all over again in creating regions and communities that work. Instead, it builds on the reality of the existing metropolis with all its complexities and contradictions. The Regional City has more to do with repair and revitalization of our existing urban and suburban environment than with creating new places.

We cannot provide a simple road map for the Regional City. Each place and time will produce a different process and a different combination of policies, designs, and laws. We have tried through examples to demonstrate a range of the possibilities. A strong governor such as Parris Glendening may use the statehouse to launch a new vision of growth. An old bit of legislation such as Oregon's UGB may be expanded into a more comprehensive regional vision. A regional planning agency such as the Puget Sound Regional Council or the Metropolitan Council in the Twin Cities may begin the process. Even litigation, such as that which led to New Jersey's fair housing, may put in place a critical element of regionalism. Civic groups such as Envision Utah, the Regional Planning Association of New York, or the Commercial Club of Chicago may lead the way.

However this effort begins, the issues of the Regional City are arising irresistibly throughout the country. We are at a turning point in the life of metropolitan America. We have outgrown the old suburban model. Virtually all aspects of metropolitan life—our population, our economy, and our ecology—are changing at an accelerating rate. The question is not *whether* our metropolitan areas are going to change but *how*. The status quo will lead us toward a continuing spiral of sprawl and inequity that will surely drag our society downward. American metropolitan regions can recapture their livability and maintain the precious qualities that we cherish in everyday life, even as they grow and change for the future.

APPENDIX

THE CHARTER OF THE NEW URBANISM

New Urbanism is a relatively recent entry into the long-standing debate about sprawl. Beginning in 1993, this movement has grown to include urban designers, architects, planners, environmentalists, economists, landscape designers, traffic engineers, elected officials, sociologists, developers, and community activists, to start an incomplete list. It represents the interests of a broad coalition of environmentalists concerned with farmland preservation, habitat enhancement, and air quality as well as inner-city advocates concerned with urban reconstruction and social equity. It weds these groups and interests with a design ethic that spans from region to building.

Put simply, the New Urbanism sees physical design—regional design, urban design, architecture, landscape design, and environmental design—as critical to the future of our communities. While recognizing that economic, social, and political issues are critical, the movement advocates attention to design. The belief is that design can play a critical role in resolving problems that governmental programs and money alone cannot.

The "new" in New Urbanism has several aspects. It is the attempt to apply the age-old principles of urbanism—diversity, street life, and human scale—to the suburb in the twenty-first century. It is also an attempt to resolve the apparent conflict between the fine grain of traditional urban environments and the large-scale realities of contemporary institutions and technologies. It is an attempt to update traditional urbanism to fit our modern lifestyles and increasingly complex economies.

The Charter of the New Urbanism specifically structures its principles at three telescoping scales: the region, the neighborhood, and the building. But perhaps most important is its assertion that the three scales are interconnected and interdependent. The Charter is simply twenty-seven principles organized by these three scales. The three elements of this book—the emerging region, the maturing suburb, and the revitalized urban neighborhood—each benefit from the principles articulated in the Charter.

The regional section of the Charter posits principles similar to those described in this book as the foundation of the Regional City. Its neighborhood-scale principles go to an urban-design philosophy that reasserts mixed-use, walkable environments. Its principles of design at the scale of the street and building seek to recreate places in which continuity and public space are reestablished for the pedestrian.

Urbanism advances the fundamental policies and goals of regionalism: that the region should be bounded, that growth should occur in more compact forms, that existing towns and cities should be revitalized, that affordable housing should be fairly distributed throughout the region, that transit should be more widespread, and that local taxes should be equitably shared. Each of these strategies is elaborated in this book as fundamental to the Regional City. Each of these strategies has become central to the larger agenda of New Urbanism.

This larger agenda gives clarity to the precarious balance at the regional scale between inner-city investments, suburban redevelopment, and the appropriate siting of greenfield development. This balance is one of the least understood aspects of New Urbanism and one of its most important. It addresses the question of where development is appropriate at the regional scale.

New Urbanism is best known (and often stereotyped) for its work at the neighborhood and town scale. At this scale the Charter's principles describe a new way of thinking about and structuring our cities and towns. Rather than the simplistic single-use zoning of most contemporary city plans, the Charter proposes a structure of three fundamental elements—neighborhoods, districts, and corridors. The Charter does not sidestep the scale of modern business and retailing. It simply calls for their placement within special districts when they are not appropriate to the scale and character of a neighborhood. In this taxonomy, the special-use district and the corridor (natural, auto, or transit) provide complements to and connections for the basic urban tissue—complete and walkable neighborhoods.

It is at the scale of the city block, its streets, and individual buildings that the test of integrating the auto and the need for more pedestrian-friendly environments is resolved. The Charter does not call for the simplistic elimination of the car, but instead challenges us to create environments that can simultaneously support walking, biking, transit, and the car. It outlines urban design strategies that reinforce human scale at the same time that they incorporate contemporary realities. Jobs no longer need to be isolated in office parks, but their integration into mixed-use neighborhoods calls for sensitive urban design. Differing types of housing no longer need buffers to separate and isolate them, but they do need an architecture that articulates a fundamental continuity within the neighborhood. Retail and civic uses do not need special zones, but they do need block, street, and building patterns that connect them to their community.

The Charter calls for an architecture that respects human scale, respects regional history and ecology, and respects the need for modesty and continuity within a physical community. Traditional architecture has much to teach us about these imperatives without prescribing nostalgic forms. And these imperatives can lead to the use of historical precedents, especially in infilling and redeveloping areas that have a strong and preestablished character. On the other hand, climate-responsive design that honors the history and culture of a place, when combined with new technologies, can lead to innovative rather than imitative design. The "seamless" integration of new and old, and a respect for existing urban patterns and scale are the imperatives of the Charter.

Too often, New Urbanism is misinterpreted simply as a conservative movement to recapture the past while ignoring the issues of our time. It is not understood as a complex system of policies and design principles that operate at multiple scales. To some, New Urbanism simply means tree-lined streets, porch-front houses, and Main Street retail—the reworking of a Norman Rockwell fantasy of small-town America, primarily for the rich.

But nostalgia is not what New Urbanism is actually proposing. Its goals and breadth are much grander, more complete and challenging. Many of the misconceptions are caused by focusing only on the neighborhood-scale prescriptions of the Charter without seeing how they are embedded in regional structures or understanding that those neighborhoods are supported by design principles at the street and building scale that attend more to environmental imperatives and urban continuities than to historical precedent.

The Charter shares its central thesis with that of this book—sprawl and social inequity must be addressed comprehensively. A fundamental tenet of the Charter speaks to the critical issue of affordability and social integration through the principles of economic diversity and inclusive neighborhoods. Economic diversity calls for a broad range of housing opportunities as well as uses within each neighborhood—affordable and expensive, small and large, rental and ownership, single and family housing. This is a very radical proposition. It implies more low-income and affordable housing in the rich suburbs at the same time that it advocates more middle-class opportunities in urban neighborhoods. It advocates mixing income groups and ethnic groups in a way that is very frightening to many communities. It is a principle that is rarely realized in practice and, given the current political climate, is almost always compromised. But it is a central tenet of the Charter and *The Regional City*—and it sets a direction quite different from most new development in the suburbs and many urban renewal programs.

New Urbanism outlines a set of design and policy principles that provide the means to reintegrate the segregated geography of our cities and suburbs. In so doing, it raises a complex set of issues. When does "economic diversity" in a distressed inner-city neighborhood become gentrification? What is the appropriate mix of inclusionary housing in a suburban town? These are tough questions that only have local answers. Gentrification may be mitigated by more affordable housing at the regional level, but what of the coherence and identity of the old neighborhood and its unique culture? There are no simple solutions. Perhaps the appropriate amount of economic diversity for a low-income neighborhood is reached when success doesn't mean moving out. Perhaps the definition for a rich neighborhood is when the schoolteacher and the fireman no longer have to drive in.

The Charter sees the physical design of a region—like the physical design of a neighborhood—as either fostering opportunities, sustainability, and diversity or inhibiting them. Such design cannot mandate a civil and vibrant culture, but it is a necessary framework. Much like healthy soil, the coherent design of a region and its neighborhoods can nurture a more equitable and robust society—or it can stunt them. This is not environmental determinism. It is simply an attempt to find a better fit between our current realities and their physical armature.

THE CHARTER

The Congress for the New Urbanism views disinvestment in central cities, the spread of placeless sprawl, increasing separation by race and income, environmental deterioration, loss of agricultural lands and wilderness, and the erosion of society's built heritage as one interrelated community building challenge.

We stand for the restoration of existing urban centers and towns within coherent metropolitan regions, the reconfiguration of sprawling suburbs into communities of real neighborhoods and diverse districts, the conservation of natural environments, and the preservation of our built legacy.

We recognize that physical solutions by themselves will not solve social and economic problems, but neither can economic vitality, community stability, and environmental health be sustained without a coherent and supportive physical framework.

We advocate the restructuring of public policy and development practices to support the following principles: neighborhoods should be diverse in use and population; communities should be designed for the pedestrian and transit as well as the car; cities and towns should be shaped by physically defined and universally accessible public spaces and community institutions; urban places should be framed by architecture and landscape design that celebrate local history, climate, ecology, and building practice.

We represent a broad-based citizenry, composed of public and private sector leaders, community activists, and multidisciplinary professionals. We are committed to reestablishing the relationship between the art of building and the making of community, through citizen-based participatory planning and design.

We dedicate ourselves to reclaiming our homes, blocks, streets, parks, neighborhoods, districts, towns, cities, regions, and environment.

We assert the following principles to guide public policy, development practice, urban planning, and design:

The Region: Metropolis, City, and Town

1. Metropolitan regions are finite places with geographic boundaries derived from topography, watersheds, coastlines, farmlands, regional parks, and river basins. The metropolis is made of multiple centers that are cities, towns, and villages, each with its own identifiable center and edges.

2. The metropolitan region is a fundamental economic unit of the contemporary world. Governmental cooperation, public policy, physical planning, and economic strategies must reflect this new reality.

3. The metropolis has a necessary and fragile relationship to its agrarian hinterland and natural landscapes. The relationship is environmental, economic, and cultural. Farmland and nature are as important to the metropolis as the garden is to the house.

4. Development patterns should not blur or eradicate the edges of the metropolis. Infill development within existing urban areas conserves environmental resources, economic investment, and social fabric, while reclaiming marginal and abandoned areas. Metropolitan regions should develop strategies to encourage such infill development over peripheral expansion.

5. Where appropriate, new development contiguous to urban boundaries should be organized as neighborhoods and districts, and be integrated with the existing urban pattern. Noncontiguous development should be organized as towns and villages with their own urban edges, and planned for a jobs/housing balance, not as bedroom suburbs.

6. The development and redevelopment of towns and cities should respect historical patterns, precedents, and boundaries.

7. Cities and towns should bring into proximity a broad spectrum of public and private uses to support a regional economy that benefits people of all incomes. Affordable housing should be distributed throughout the region to match job opportunities and to avoid concentrations of poverty.

8. The physical organization of the region should be supported by a framework of transportation alternatives. Transit, pedestrian, and bicycle systems should maximize access and mobility throughout the region while reducing dependence upon the automobile.

9. Revenues and resources can be shared more cooperatively among the municipalities and centers within regions to avoid destructive competition for tax base and to promote rational coordination of transportation, recreation, public services, housing, and community institutions.

The Neighborhood, the District, and the Corridor

1. The neighborhood, the district, and the corridor are the essential elements of development and redevelopment in the metropolis. They form identifiable areas that encourage citizens to take responsibility for their maintenance and evolution.

2. Neighborhoods should be compact, pedestrian friendly, and mixed use. Districts generally emphasize a special single use, and should follow the principles of neighborhood design when possible. Corridors are regional connectors of neighborhoods and districts; they range from boulevards and rail lines to rivers and parkways.

3. Many activities of daily living should occur within walking distance, allowing independence to those who do not drive, especially the elderly and the young. Interconnected networks of streets should be designed to encourage walking, reduce the number and length of automobile trips, and conserve energy.

4. Within neighborhoods, a broad range of housing types and price levels can bring people of diverse ages, races, and incomes into daily interaction, strengthening the personal and civic bonds essential to an authentic community.

5. Transit corridors, when properly planned and coordinated, can help organize metropolitan structure and revitalize urban centers. In contrast, highway corridors should not displace investment from existing centers.

6. Appropriate building densities and land uses should be within walking distance of transit stops, permitting public transit to become a viable alternative to the automobile.

7. Concentrations of civic, institutional, and commercial activity should be embedded in neighborhoods and districts, not isolated in remote, single-use complexes. Schools should be sized and located to enable children to walk or bicycle to them.

8. The economic health and harmonious evolution of neighborhoods, districts, and corridors can be improved through graphic urban design codes that serve as predictable guides for change.

9. A range of parks, from tot-lots and village greens to ballfields and community gardens, should be distributed within neighborhoods. Conservation areas and open lands should be used to define and connect different neighborhoods and districts.

The Block, the Street, and the Building

1. A primary task of all urban architecture and landscape design is the physical definition of streets and public spaces as places of shared use.

2. Individual architectural projects should be seamlessly linked to their surroundings. This issue transcends style.

3. The revitalization of urban places depends on safety and security. The design of streets and buildings should reinforce safe environments, but not at the expense of accessibility and openness.

4. In the contemporary metropolis, development must adequately accommodate automobiles. It should do so in ways that respect the pedestrian and the form of public space.

5. Streets and squares should be safe, comfortable, and interesting to the pedestrian. Properly configured, they encourage walking and enable neighbors to know each other and protect their communities.

6. Architecture and landscape design should grow from local climate, topography, history, and building practice.

7. Civic buildings and public gathering places require important sites to reinforce community identity and the culture of democracy. They deserve distinctive form, because their role is different from that of other buildings and places that constitute the fabric of the city.

8. All buildings should provide their inhabitants with a clear sense of location, weather, and time. Natural methods of heating and cooling can be more resource-efficient than mechanical systems.

9. Preservation and renewal of historic buildings, districts, and landscapes affirm the continuity and evolution of urban society.

PROJECT CREDITS

The illustrative plans shown in the color plates are selected from Calthorpe Associate's projects. There are many other available examples—so many, in fact, that the task of reviewing and selecting from others' works seemed overwhelming. This abundance is, of course, a blessing and a vindication that many of the ideas expressed here are becoming more and more commonplace. The plans are intended to illustrate certain ideas and possibilities. Some have been built, some have been modified before realization, some are still in process, some have been abandoned, and some (the case studies) were only intended to illustrate and educate. The selection criteria was to demonstrate the design philosophy in as many different scales and contexts as possible.

In addition, each project is a product of a large design and consultant team as well as an extensive community process. The community process in each case involved a hands-on workshop technique in which the participants were provided the tools to make their own designs, to struggle with the trade-offs, and to work as teams instead of as special interest groups. The credits for each project follow.

plate	*project*	*date*	*client*	*team*	*illustrations*
PORTLAND					
CLACKAMAS	Region 2040	1994	Metro	**Calthorpe Associates**	C. Tolon, Mark Mack
HILLSDALE				*(for all Portland projects)*	C. Tolon, Mark Mack
ORENCO				*Shelley Poticha (PM), Joey Scanga,*	C. Tolon, Mark Mack
BEAVERTON				*Matt Taecker, Sue Chan,*	Mark Mack
				Catherine Chang, Tom Ford	
UTAH					
REGIONAL	Envision Utah	2000	Coalition for	**Calthorpe Associates**	
PLANS			Utah's Future	*Joe DiStefano (PM)*	
				Fregonese Calthorpe Associates	
PROVO	Intermodal	1999	Provo City	**Calthorpe Associates**	Thomas Prosek
	Corridor Plan			*Tim Rood (PM), Redger Hodges*	
WEST VALLEY	Jordan River	1999	West Valley City	**Calthorpe Associates**	Thomas Prosek
CITY	Neighborhood			*Tim Rood (PM), David Blake,*	
	Plan			*Kathryn Clark*	
CENTERVILLE	Town Center Plan	1999	Centerville City	**Calthorpe Associates**	Thomas Prosek
				Tim Rood (PM), David Blake,	
				Kathryn Clark	
SANDY/MIDVALE	Sandy/Midvale	1999	Sandy City and	**Calthorpe Associates**	Thomas Prosek
	Transit Oriented		Midvale City	*Tim Rood (PM), Danno Glanz*	
	Development Plan			*Chad Johnston*	
GREY/GREENFIELDS					
BAY MEADOWS	Bay Meadows	1997	California	**Calthorpe Associates**	Thomas Prosek
	Specific Plan		Jockey Club	*Bruce Fukuji (PM), Danno Glanz,*	
				Sue Chan, Matt Taecker, Clark Williams	
				Fehr & Peers: Traffic	
				Brian Kangas Foulk: Civil Engineering	
				Ken Kay Associates: Landscape Architecture	

(PM) Project Manager

plate	project	date	client	team	illustrations
STAPLETON	Stapleton Airport Redevelopment Plan	2000	Forest City Stapleton	**Calthorpe Associates** *Danno Glanz, Rodger Hodges, David Blake, Tim Rood* **BRW, Antero, Matrix:** Civil Engineering **EDAW:** Landscape Architecture **KA Architecture, Cox, Wolff Lyon, Urban Design Group, Johnson Fain:** Architecture	Stanley Doctor
MOFFETT FIELD	Vision Plan for NASA Ames	1998	NASA Ames	**Calthorpe Associates** *Joey Scanga (PM), Danno Glanz, Hillary Bidwell* **Arcadia Land Company:** Developers **Fehr & Peers:** Traffic	Thomas Prosek
NORTHAMPTON	Northampton State Hospital Redevelopment Plan	2000	Community Builders	**Calthorpe Associates** *Matt Taecker (PM), Roger Hodges*	Thomas Prosek
HIGHLAND'S GARDEN VILLAGE	Highland's Garden Village	2000	Affordable Housing Development Corp.	**Calthorpe Associates** *Joey Scanga (PM), Kathryn Clark, David Blake, Roger Hodges, Chad Johnston, Danno Glanz, Tom Ford* **Lee Weintraub:** Landscape Architecture **OZ Architecture:** Architecture **Civitas:** Zoning and Entitlements	
THE CROSSINGS	The Crossings Neighborhood Plan	1995	TPG Development Corporation	**Calthorpe Associates** *Joey Scanga (PM), Matt Taecker (PM, Phase 1), Danno Glanz, Tom Ford, Cleve Brakefield, Clark Williams* **HST Architects:** Apartment Architecture **Guzzardo and Associates, Gary Strand:** Landscape Architecture **Sandis Humber Jones:** Civil Engineering	
UNIVERSITY AVE.	University Avenue Strategic Plan	1996	City of Berkeley	**Calthorpe Associates** *Shelly Poticha (PM), Danno Glanz, Pietro Calogero, Catherine Chang, Isabelle Duvivier* **Bay Area Economics:** Market Analysis	

(PM) Project Manager

Project Credits

plate	project	date	client	team	illustrations
AGGIE VILLAGE	First Street & Aggie Village Master Plan and Design Objectives	1993	University of California at Davis	**Calthorpe Associates** *Philip Erickson (PM), Joey Scanga* **Bob Segar, Campus Planner:** Residential Masterplan **Pyramid Construction:** Architect/Builder **Mark Dziewulski Architect:** Retail Architect **Fulcrum Capital:** Retail Developer	
ST. CROIX	The St. Croix Valley Development Design Study	2000	Metropolitan Council	**Calthorpe Associates** *Tim Rood (PM), Diana Marsh,* *Joe DiStefano, Ariella Granett* **Urban Advantage:** Photo Simulations	Steve Price
ONTARIO MOUNTAIN AVENUE	Mountain Village Specific Plan	1997	City of Ontario, Ontario Redevelopment Agency	**Calthorpe Associates** *Matt Taecker (PM), David Blake,* *Roger Hodges, Sue Chan,* *Danno Glanz, Bruce Fukuji*	Thomas Prosek
PALO ALTO	Palo Alto Plan	1994	City of Palo Alto	**Calthorpe Associates** *Shelley Poticha, Catherine Chang,* *Tom Ford, Joe Scanga,* *Elizabeth Gourley* **Economic & Planning Systems:** Fiscal Analysis **MIG:** Public Involvement and Planning	
ISSAQUAH	Issaquah Highlands	2000	Port Blakely Communities	**Calthorpe Associates** *David Blake (PM), Kathryn Clark* *Shunji Suzuki, John Beutler* *John Moynahan, Chad Johnston* **Fehr and Peers:** Traffic **David Evans and Associates, Inc.:** Civil Engineering	Thomas Prosek
SE ORLANDO	Southeast Orlando Development Plan Development Guidelines and Standards	1997	City of Orlando	**Calthorpe Associates** *David Blake, Joey Scanga,* *Clark Williams,* *Philip Erickson (PM)* *Shelley Poticha (PM)* **Glatting Jackson Anglin** **Lopez Rinehart, Inc.:** Transportation **Economic & Planning Systems:** Market and Fiscal Analysis **Market Perspectives:** Market Analysis **WBQ Engineering:** Civil Engineering **Lotspeich and Associates, Inc.:** Land Use, Law	

(PM) Project Manager

plate	*project*	*date*	*client*	*team*	*illustrations*
URBAN REVITALIZATION					
HOLYOKE/ CHURCHILL	Churchill Neighborhood Revitalization Plan	1999	Holyoke Housing Authority The Community Builders	**Calthorpe Associates** *Matt Taecker (PM), Danno Glanz, Shelly Poticha* **Dietz & Co.:** Architecture **Denig Design:** Landscape Architecture	Dietz Architecture
CURTIS PARK	Curtis Park Hope VI Housing	2000	Housing Authority of the City and County of Denver Integral Development Corporation	**Calthorpe Associates** *Joey Scanga (PM), Chad Johnston, Danno Glanz* **Abo-Copeland:** Architect of Record **Wong Strauch Architecture:** Architecture **THK Associates, Inc.:** Landscape Architecture **Martin & Martin:** Civil Engineering	Thomas Prosek
COATESVILLE	Neighborhood Revitalization Plan	1998	Housing Authority of the County of Chester Pennsylvania The Community Builders	**Calthorpe Associates** *Joey Scanga (PM), Danno Glanz, Matt Taecker, Clark Williams* **Kelly/Maiello Inc.:** Architecture	
HORNER	Horner Neighborhood Plan	1995	Chicago Housing Authority	**Calthorpe Associates** *Joey Scanga, Matt Taecker, Tom Ford* **The Habitat Co.:** Development Consultants **Solomon Cordwell Buenz & Associates:** Architecture	
NEWPORT	North End Revitalization Plan	1999	City of Newport Rhode Island	**Calthorpe Associates** *Matt Taecker (PM), John Beutler, John Moynahan, Danno Glanz, Tom Ford* **Newport Collaborative Architects:** Architecture	
NOMA	North of Massachusetts Avenue (NoMa) Redevelopment Plan	2000	Cultural Development Corporation	**Calthorpe Associates** *Joey Scanga* **Urban Design Associates:** Urban Planning and Architecture **Economic Research Associates:** Market and Fiscal Analysis	Urban Design Associates

(PM) Project Manager

BIBLIOGRAPHY

Much of the source material used in writing this book is based on the firsthand knowledge and experience of the authors. The details of the Portland and Salt Lake City case studies were drawn from the experience of Calthorpe & Associates in working in both those locations. Most of the rest of the location-specific material was gathered by William Fulton, either as part of other journalistic or research efforts or specifically for this book. Many of the sources are included in the bibliographic list below.

Introduction

Benfield, F. Kaid, Matthew D. Raimi, and Donald D. T. Chen, *Once There Were Greenfields: How Urban Sprawl Is Undermining America's Environment, Economy and Social Fabric.* Washington, DC: Natural Resources Defense Council, 1999.

Garreau, Joel, *Edge City: Life on the New Frontier.* New York: Doubleday, 1991.

Chapter 1: Living in the Regional World

Altshuler, Alan, William Morrill, Harold Wolman, and Faith Mitchell (eds.), *Governance and Opportunity in Metropolitan America.* Washington, DC: National Academy Press, 1999.

Barnes, William H., and Larry Ledebur, *The New Regional Economics: The U.S. Common Market and the Global Economy.* Newbury Park, CA: Sage Publishing, 1997.

Cisneros, Henry G. (ed.), *Interwoven Destinies: Cities and the Nation.* New York: Norton, 1993.

Downs, Anthony, *New Visions for Metropolitan America.* Washington, DC: The Brookings Institution, 1995.

Fulton, William, and Paul Shigley. "Operation Desert Sprawl: The biggest issue in booming Las Vegas isn't growth. It's finding somebody to pay the staggering costs of growth." *Governing,* Vol. XII, No XI (August 1999), pp. 16–21.

Katz, Bruce, *Reflections on Regionalism.* Washington, DC: The Brookings Institution, 2000.

Leopold, Aldo, *A Sand County Almanac.* New York: Ballantine Books, 1991 (originally published 1949).

Lewis, Sinclair, *Main Street.* Mineola, NY: Dover Publications, 1999 (originally published 1920).

Ohmae, Kenichi, *The End of the Nation State: The Rise of Regional Economies.* New York: Free Press, 1995.

Orfield, Myron, *Metropolitics: A Regional Agenda for Community and Stability.* Washington, DC: The Brookings Institution, 1997.

Partners for Livable Communities, *The Livable City: Revitalizing Urban Communities.* New York: McGraw-Hill, 2000.

Pastor, Manuel, Peter Dreier, J. Eugene Grigsby III, and Marta Lopez-Graza, *Regions That Work: How Cities and Suburbs Can Grow Together.* Minneapolis: University of Minnesota Press, 2000.

Stein, Clarence S., *Toward New Towns for America,* with an introduction by Lewis Mumford. Cambridge, MA: MIT Press, 1957, 1989.

Storper, Michael, *The Regional World: Territorial Development in a Global Economy.* New York: Guilford Press, 1997.

Chapter 2: Communities of Place

Boorstin, Daniel J., *The Americans: The National Experience.* New York: Random House, 1988 (originally published 1974).

Burchell, Robert, et al., "Costs of Sprawl Revisited: The Evidence of Sprawl's Negative and Positive Impacts," Transportational Research Board and National Research Council. Washington, DC: National Academy Press, 1997.

Calthorpe, Peter, *The Next American Metropolis: Ecology, Community, and the American Dream.* Princeton, NJ: Princeton Architectural Press, 1993.

Jacobs, Jane, *The Death and Life of Great American Cities.* New York: Vintage Books, 1993 (originally published 1961).

Oldenburg, Ray, *The Great Good Place: Cafes, Coffee Shops, Bookstores, Bars, Hair Salons, and Other Hangouts at the Heart of a Community.* New York: Marlowe & Co., 1999 (originally published 1991).

Putnam, Robert D., *Bowling Alone: The Collapse and Revival of American Community.* New York: Simon & Schuster, 2000.

VanderRyn, Sim, and Peter Calthorpe, *Sustainable Communities: A New Design Synthesis for Cities, Suburbs, and Towns.* San Francisco: Sierra Club Books, 1991.

Whyte, William H., *City: Rediscovering the Center.* New York: Doubleday, 1988.

Chapter 3: Designing the Region

Leccese, Michael, and Kathleen McCormick (eds.). Charter of the New Urbanism. New York: McGraw-Hill Professional Publishing, 1999.

Chapter 4: Public Policy and the Regional City

Burchell, Robert W., *Impact Assessment of the New Jersey State Development and Redevelopment Plan,* New Jersey State Planning Commission, June 1992.

Eppli, Mark J., and Charles C. Tu, *Valuing the New Urbanism: The Impact of the New Urbanism on Prices of Single-Family Homes.* Washington, DC: Urban Land Institute, 1999.

JHK & Associates, *Transportation-Related Land Use Strategies to Minimize Motor Vehicle Emissions: An Indirect Source Research Study,* final report to the California Air Resources Board, Chapters 1–7, June 1995.

Norquist, John O., *The Wealth of Cities: Revitalizing the Centers of American Life.* Reading, MA: Addison-Wesley Longman, 1998.

Rosenbaum, James, "Changing the Geography of Opportunity by Expanding Residential Choice: Lessons from the *Gautreaux* Program." *Housing Policy Debate,* Vol. VI, No. 1 (1995), pp. 231–269.

Staley, Samuel R., and Gerard C. S. Mildner, "Urban-growth Boundaries and Housing Affordability: Lessons from Portland." *Reason Public Policy Institute Policy Brief,* October 1999 (Brief No. 11).

Traub, James, "What No School Can Do." *The New York Times Magazine,* January 16, 2000. pp. 52–57, 68, 81, 90–91.

Chapter 5: The Federal Role in Regionalism

Federal National Mortgage Association, 1999 Information Statement, www.fanniemae.com/markets/debt/w21804.html#000.

Horan, Tom, Hank Dittmar, and Daniel R. Jordan, "ISTEA and the Transformation in U.S. Transportation Policy: Sustainable Communities from a Federal Initiative." Working paper, Claremont Graduate University Research Institute, 1997.

Chapter 6: Designing the Regions: Portland, Salt Lake City, and Seattle

Blizzard, Meeky, *Creating Better Communities: The LUTRAQ Principles.* Portland: Sensible Transportation Options for People and 1000 Friends of Oregon, 1996.

Calthorpe Associates, Envision Utah: Producing a Vision for the Future of the Greater Wasatch Area, April 1999.

Calthorpe Associates, Region 2040. May 1994.

Cambridge Systematics, Inc. with Hague Consulting Group, "Making the Land Use Transportation, Air Quality Connection: Modeling Practices." Portland, OR: 1000 Friends of Oregon, October 1991 (Vol. I).

Committee to Study Housing Affordability, Oregon Housing Cost Study, final report, December 1998.

"Concepts for Growth: Report to Council," Metro, June 1994.

Dyett, Blayney, et al., "Making the Land Use, Transportation, Air Quality Connection: Implementation." Portland, OR: 1000 Friends of Oregon, October 1995 (Vol. VI).

ECONorthwest with Free and Associates, Greater Wasatch Area Housing Analysis, September 1999.

Fulton, William: "Ring Around the Region: It's Better than Latte, Say Fans of Washington's Nine-Year-Old Growth Management Law," *Planning Magazine* (Vol. LXV, No. III (March 1999), pp. 18–21.

Hinshaw, Mark, *Citistate Seattle: Shaping a Modern Metropolis.* Chicago: APA Press, 1999.

"Making the Connections: A summary of the LUTRAQ project." Portland, OR: 1000 Friends of Oregon, February 1997 (Vol. VII).

Parsons Brinckerhoff Quade, and Douglas, Inc., et al., "Making the Land Use, Transportation, Air Quality Connection: The Pedestrian Environment." Portland, OR: 1000 Friends of Oregon, December 1993 (Vol. IVA).

Parsons Brinckerhoff Quade, and Douglas, Inc., et al., "Making the Land Use, Transportation, Air Quality Connection: Building Orientation," supplement to Vol. IVA. Portland, OR: 1000 Friends of Oregon, May 1994 (Vol. IVB).

Pivo, Gary, "Regional Efforts to Achieve Sustainability in Seattle: Skinny Latte or Double Fat Mocha?" Prepared for the Creating Sustainable Places Symposium,

College of Architecture and Environmental Design, Arizona State University, January 1998.

Phillips, Justin, and Eban Goodstein, "Has Portland's Urban Growth Boundary Raised Housing Prices?" Draft, presented at Western Economics Association Meeting, June 1998.

Portland Metro, Regional Framework Plan, June 1997.

PricewaterhouseCoopers and Lend Lease Real Estate Investments, Emerging Trends in Real Estate 2000, 1999.

Puget Sound Regional Council, "Regional Review: Monitoring Change in the Central Puget Sound Region." Seattle, WA: Puget Sound Regional Council, September 1997.

Puget Sound Regional Council, "Vision 2020: 1995 Update," May 25, 1995.

Quality Growth Efficiency Tools Technical Committee, "Scenario Analysis." Salt Lake City: Governor's Office of Planning and Budget, 1999.

"Regional Urban Growth Goals and Objectives," Ordinance No. 95-625A. Metro, 1995.

"Under Construction: Building a Livable Future: Summaries of Regional Transportation and Land Use Projects." *Tri-Met,* May 1996.

Wallace Stegner Center for Land, Resource and the Environment, "Transportation, Land Use and Ecology along the Wasatch Front." Salt lake City, UT: University of Utah College of Law, 1999.

Chapter 7: The Superregions: New York, Chicago, and San Francisco

Chicago Land Transportation and Air Quality Commission, *The $650 Billion Decision: The Chicago Transportation Plan for Northeastern Illinois,* abridged version. Chicago: Center for Neighborhood Technology, 1995.

Fulton, William, *The Reluctant Metropolis: The Politics of Urban Growth in Los Angeles.* Point Arena, CA: Solano Press Books, 1997.

Johnson, Elmer, "Chicago Metropolis 2020: Preparing Metropolitan Chicago for the 21st Century." A project of the Commercial Club of Chicago in association with the American Academy of Arts & Sciences, 1998.

Peirce, Neal R., and Jerry Hagstrom, *The Book of America: Inside the Fifty States Today.* New York: Warner Books, 1984.

Scott, Mel, *The San Francisco Bay Area: A Metropolis in Perspective,* second edition. Berkeley: University of California Press, 1985.

Urban Ecology Inc., *Blueprint for a Sustainable Bay Area.* Oakland: Urban Ecology, 1996.

Wunch, James, The Regional Plan at Seventy: An Interpretation, unpublished paper, 1999.

Yaro, Robert D., and Tony Hiss, *A Region at Risk: The Third Regional Plan for the New York–New Jersey–Connecticut Metropolitan Area.* Washington, DC: Island Press, 1996.

Chapter 8: State-Led Regionalism: Florida, Maryland, and Minnesota

Adams, John S., and Barbara J. VanDrasek, *Minneapolis–St. Paul: People, Places, and Public Life.* Minneapolis: The University of Minnesota Press, 1993.

Calthorpe Associates, The St. Croix Valley Development Design Study, January 2000.

Ehrenhalt, Alan, "The Czar of Gridlock: Terrified of Becoming the Next Los Angeles, the Atlanta Region Has Given a Superagency Controlled by the Governor Dictatorial Powers to Regulate Traffic, Smog, and Sprawl." *Governing,* Vol. XII, No. VIII (May 1999), pp. 20–27.

Maryland Office of Planning, Smart Growth and Neighborhood Conservation.

Mondale, Ted, "Maintaining Our Competitive Advantage in the 21st Century." State of the Region Address, March 29, 1999.

Transportation and Land Use Study Committee, Final Report on Land Use and Transportation Planning in Florida, January 15, 1999.

Chapter 9: The Suburb's Maturation

Calthorpe Associates, et al., Southeast Orlando Development Plan: Development Guideline and Standards, October 1997.

Calthorpe Associates Consulting Team, Sonoma/Marin: Multi-Modal Transportation and Land Use Study: Final Report, June 1997.

Fehr and Peers Associates, Inc., Issaquah Highlands Operations Analysis Report, June 1998.

Henke, Cliff, "U.S. Begins Second Light Rail Revolution." *Metro Magazine,* November/December 1999, pp. 40–46.

Hirschhorn, Joel S., "Growing Pains: Quality of Life in the New Economy." Washington, DC: National Governors' Association, 2000.

Chapter 10: Renewing Urban Neighborhoods

Cisneros, Henry G., *The Transformation of America's Public Housing: A Status Report.* Washington, DC: U.S. Department of Housing and Urban Development, 1996.

Cisneros, Henry G., "Regionalism: The New Geography of Opportunity." Unpublished essay, 1995.

Congress for New Urbanism, The, "Principles for Inner City Neighborhood Design: HOPE VI and the New Urbanism." Washington, DC: The Congress for New Urbanism and U.S. Department of Housing and Urban Design, 2000.

Gratz, Roberta Brandes, *The Living City: How Americ's Cities Are Being Revitalized by Thinking Big in a Small Way.* New York: John Wiley and Sons, 1994.

Gratz, Roberta Brandes, and Norman Mintz, *Cities Back from the Edge: New Life for Downtown.* New York: John Wiley and Sons, 1998.

U.S. Department of Housing and Urban Development and the American Institute of Architects, *Vision/Reality: Strategies for Community Change.* Washington, DC: U.S. Department of Housing and Urban Development, March 1994.

U.S. Department of Housing and Urban Development, Office of Policy Development and Research, Moving to Opportunity Fair Housing Demonstration Program: Current Status and Initial Findings, September 1999.

INDEX

Italicized page numbers refer to illustrations.